"An inspiration for all entrepreneurs—Fiona demonstrates that if you follow your dreams and believe in yourself you can accomplish great things!"
Joanne Johnson, Co-Founder - Robustion Technologies Inc.

"Fiona arrived at entrepreneurship through a non-traditional way, and hearing her story and all the barriers she had to overcome was inspiring."
HUB Ottawa, Jan 13, 2013

"Fiona successfully matches business savvy and an ability to foresee opportunities with motherhood and philanthropy. Her fierce commitment to encouraging entrepreneurialism makes her a brilliant role model for women."
Jennifer MacKinnon, CEO – Felix

"Offers readers a unique perspective on entrepreneurship from a successful female founder."
David Coletto, Abacus Data

"Fiona is a tireless entrepreneur and a true champion for women entrepreneurs in all disciplines. Her hard earned experience, successful exit and advisory roles to start-ups make her an excellent mentor to learn from. Her book will

provide excellent lessons for others—men or women—wanting to become entrepreneurs."
Dr. Sue Abu-Hakima, Co-Founder/CEO - Amika Mobile Corp.

"An extraordinary visionary and leader. Over the course of her leadership, she built the largest private sector trauma services business in Canada."
Kathy MacLeod - Trauma Care Network

"Ms. Gilligan devotes her life to the support, encouragement and mentoring of other Female Founders and has been instrumental in the success of countless businesses and individuals."
Andi Marcus, CEO, Mistura Beauty

"It's always a pleasure to work with Fiona. Her dedication to Startup Festival has been great. She cares...a lot...and it shows."
Philippe Telio, Founder - StartUp Festival

"An incredibly 'real' trailblazer and role model to young women entrepreneurs, Fiona proves that you can be a successful entrepreneur capable of constant reinvention of yourself, a loving single Mother and a leader in the community."
Vivian Prokop, Former CEO – Canadian Youth Business Foundation

Confessions *of a* *Girl*PRENEUR

Best Wishes!

Fiona

Confessions *of a* *Girl*PRENEUR

Life, Love, Business and Babies

Fiona Gilligan
with Kendall McQueen

Arranmore Publishing

Confessions *of a Girl*PRENEUR

C 2014. All rights reserved

Published by Arranmore Publishers

No part of this book may be used or reproduced in any manner without the prior written permission of Arranmore Publishers, except in the case of brief quotations embedded in a review.

With the exception of the author's, all names have been changed to protect privacy. All stories in the business case study section are based on fictitious characters and companies.

This book is written as a memoir in combination with business and entre-preneur information. In no way should this book be considered a defini-tive guide to business.

Arranmore Publishing books may be purchased for educational, business or promotional use through www.fionagilligan.com

Library and Archives Canada Cataloguing in Publication information is available.

ISBN: 1500672270
ISBN 13: 9781500672270

Confessions of a GirlPRENEUR is printed on 100% post-consumer waste paper.

Printed and bound in Canada

Acknowledgements

Confessions of a GirlPRENEUR is a special project, and I am very grateful to Kendall McQueen for bringing her talents as a writer to this book and for her ability and determination to find my essential story.

I have many people in my life to be thankful for, and as such, I cannot possibly name you all. To each and every one of you, a heartfelt thank you. Without my family and friends, I would not be who I am today.

To all the GirlPreneurs and Entrepreneurs out there who have encouraged me to publish my story, thank you. You are the best!

And to you the reader, thank you for picking up this book. We are grateful for your time and hope it will inspire, motivate and entertain you.

To my girls, Ciara and Siobhán, I love you more than all the stars in the Universe. And to my Mother and Father, who had the love and patience to raise a spirited Girl child.

Contents

Introduction		xiii
Chapter 1:	The Crow in the Bag	1
Chapter 2:	Popularity is Overrated	12
Chapter 3:	The Beauty of Brevity	20
Chapter 4:	The Game	26
Chapter 5:	Drifting	30
Chapter 6:	Up in the Air	35
Chapter 7:	Sitting on a Rock	42
Chapter 8:	Career Code-Blue	46
Chapter 9:	Getting Launched	51
Chapter 10:	Peter	57
Chapter 11:	Love What You Do	64

Chapter 12: Becoming Financially Savvy — 73

Chapter 13: Bootstrapping Your Business — 78

Chapter 14: Your First Year in Business — 83

Chapter 15: Shout Out — 92

Chapter 16: And Now…
Putting it all Together — 99

Chapter 17: The Idea Phase — 101

Chapter 18: The Goal-Setting Phase — 111

Chapter 19: Your Business Plan — 119

Chapter 20: The Art of Marketing
and Sales — 126

Chapter 21: A GirlPreneur's Trade Secrets
in Marketing and Sales — 136

Chapter 22: The Confessions — 139

Afterword — 159

Introduction

As a GirlPreneur, you are the largest untapped economic resource on our planet. Women entre-preneurs are as unique and varied as the ideas, products and services we bring to the marketplace, yet we all share many common traits, dreams and challenges.

As an aspiring GirlPreneur, you can change the ecosystem. Whether you want to start a small home-based cake decorating business or build a car parts empire, either way, by applying creativity to solve the problems that your business addresses, you are innovating. You are changing the way we do things. You might be inventing computer apps, or organizing bike tours, whatever it is, by starting an enterprise in your local ecosystem that addresses concerns, or improves upon some service or prod-uct, you are working to benefit your community, your family and yourself.

My journey to becoming an entrepreneur began many years before I started my first busi-ness. Some of the reasons I would go on to start a company were grounded in my upbringing and what I saw out there in the world as a young girl. Opening a business is a series of acts, but becoming a GirlPreneur is a lifelong process. This is the story of how that process unfolded for me, but I think many aspiring women entrepreneurs will see a little of themselves in the young girl who once traded a pack of gum for a crow.

This is also a story about beating the odds; about how I went from being an unemployed social worker to starting my own business. It is about how I followed my passion and turned what started as a small private practice into an industry-leading company.

But more importantly, it is a story about a regular girl who grows up and doesn't forget what her father taught her all those years ago when she didn't feel like doing something. "Get your boots on!" was his motto. Just get out there and do what needs doing was the main message throughout my childhood. This book couldn't have been written without the solid grounding I had from my family. I learned how to not be afraid to take chances and to believe in myself. This is also a story about discovering that sometimes when we come to a crossroads, it can be an opportunity in disguise. Letting go of the supposed safety net of employment to carve out a path as an entrepreneur was one of the best decisions that I ever made.

Few things match waking up every day to do what you love, to be your own boss and to work harder than you've ever worked. Because as entrepreneurs, we don't distinguish work from life. Our life is our work. We all have the passion, persistence and smarts needed to become successful entrepreneurs, but only if we are willing to take a chance on ourselves and make it happen.

This book was written to inspire, encourage, and motivate the aspiring GirlPreneur. Entrepreneurship can be a great career choice. There is no secret formula nor must you be born with special talents, you only need a passion for something, the determination to make it happen, the persistence to see it through, and the willingness to learn from the school of life. In addition to my own story you will also find case scenarios based upon the real stories of other successful GirlPreneurs that will highlight some of the principles to consider before, during and after venturing into business.

We are delighted and honoured that you have picked up a copy of *Confessions of a GirlPRENEUR*. Our hope is that you will see yourself and your potential in this story and that when you close up this book, you will believe that you can do anything you put your mind to. All you need to do is, "Get your boots on!"

GirlPreneur, your time is now!

The Crow in the Bag

Remember all those funny things you did as a kid, what curious and interesting things would pop into your head as you were out running around the neighborhood. You would see birds in the sky, play chase with your dog, jump over fences, find a friend around the corner or happen onto a frog jumping across the path. All those things would form the picture of your day. When your mom asked you how your day was, that picture would flash up like a photo in front of your face and you'd say, "Fine." Even if you'd stumbled over the frog, been teased by the friend, or lost the dog's ball. As a kid, you learned early to accept the chaos with the calm. It was part of life's early lessons. But life seemed always new and unpredictable. The days were long, the moments with friends even longer, the impression was that time was everlasting and that you could always do your homework later.

If we take a look back at our childhoods and risk exploring all those hazy memories of our youth, we can often trace the journey we've made to get where we are today and sometimes be surprised by our strength and marvel at the courage it took to brave those years. So, I would like to start by telling you a bit about myself and take you on my journey to becoming a GirlPreneur.

Let me tell you about my first business transaction.

I was six years old and I was sitting on top of a hydro box on Osborne Street in Old Ottawa South with my friend Rosey. My mom had just bought me a pack of fruity gum—something she never did. But a few days earlier she had caught me scraping old gum off the road and when I proceeded to pop it into my mouth, little rocks and all, I suppose she figured she had better give in a little.

So there I was with a prized yellow pack in my hand, kicking my legs against the hot metal, when along came another friend, Frankey. In one fist, he was carrying a dirty old paper bag. "What's in it?" I asked. He grinned up at me with a big tooth-less grin and slowly opened the bag. Feathers blew out everywhere. "Crow," he said, nonchalantly. I stared into the bag, trying to see through all those black feathers, not believing him but not sure. "Is it dead?" I ventured, the idea of it piqu-ing my interest. Frankey nodded. "Do ya want it?" he asked, eyeing me. I looked down at him. Rosey was still staring with big round eyes at the bag. A few feathers blew out in small wisps like in a magic show. One landed on my finger, "You don't want

Confessions of a GirlPRENEUR | 3

it?" I asked. He stared at me, at the bag, then at Rosey, and said, "Nah, you can have it." "Sure," I declared, "I'll take it."

My first business transaction, a dead crow, but I felt I'd gotten the better deal. Maybe it was the magic of floating feathers, maybe it was the mystery of that bird dead in the bag, like in those nursery tales of dead things, potentially wicked. At any rate, Frankey had been eyeing the sticks of gum now clenched firmly in my fist. So I wasn't particularly surprised when he added, "But ya gotta give me the pack for the crow."

I gave Frankey the pack and took the crow. I slid off the hydro box, said goodbye to Rosey and went home alone, carrying the bag.

Of course, later that afternoon when my mother discovered it, she gasped and grabbed the bag out of my hands. Not only did I lose the gum and the crow, but I had to take a hot shower and scrub off any escapees from among the crow maggots that had eluded my attention but not my mom's. And I hated showers.

All I felt at that moment was that even though I'd never see those shiny black feathers atop my box of charms, it didn't matter because I'd had the thrill of the exchange. That trade was the first of many swaps, exchanges and barters through the years between me and the neighborhood kids.

Swapping something of mine for something of theirs seemed a good deal. Old things made new again. But my mom sometimes thought I'd gotten the short end of the stick and would remind me that I might want to consider more carefully the value of what I'd be losing versus what I'd be gaining.

I was lucky. I had rock star parents. Not the kind that perform on a stage, but the kind who knew how to pick themselves up after a fall, dust themselves off and move on. My mom grew up in Ireland in a big Catholic family. Her father died when she was young and her mother raised six kids in a small town. My grandmother kept the family store open, even though back then women rarely ran businesses on their own. My grandmother felt it was important to educate her girls, so despite the family barely scraping by, my mother went to university and got a bachelor's degree. Then, wanting to move out of small-town Ireland, she moved to London and became a flight attendant for British Airways. Yes, back when they had to wear pillbox hats and pencil skirts, and remain unmarried in order to keep their jobs. You see I come from a line of strong female role models who had no choice but to buck trends, work hard and make their own opportunities in a man's world.

My mother took that job because she wanted to see the world. She did. What she also saw was my dad, who happened to be sitting six rows up

Confessions of a GirlPRENEUR | 5

from her at a soccer match in London one fine spring day. He was a Canadian pilot flying back from Cairo, and they met at that match because my father caught her eye and—meeting her for the first time—teasingly asked, "Will you marry me?" Audacious but, as it turned out, sincere. And she couldn't resist the handsome guy with a certain sparkle in his eye. They dated for six months, traveling back and forth between Egypt and England. Then my mother gave up her job to follow love and opportunity to another country. She got on a boat and crossed the Atlantic, landing in Halifax, Nova Scotia, then boarded a train to his home base of Ottawa, Ontario and arrived before Christmas.

Looking back I can see many of the personality traits that made me a natural entrepreneur were the result of influences from my childhood. I was raised by two strong people: adventurous, unafraid and with deeply-held beliefs in hard work. I suppose my mom could be called an early feminist; she was politicized at a young age by having a widowed mother who worked and ran a business. My father was the same, having seen his mother go through many hardships while raising four children on her own.

My mom taught kindergarten for 25 years. This was the job she had trained for in England before she was a flight attendant, and the one she chose to make her career after moving to Canada. My parents settled in Ottawa. My brother was born a year later and I came along two years after him. My mother tells me that, although she was in love, it was difficult to be far away from family and friends. As a pilot, my father was away much of the time. Not only did my mom work all day and raise two kids, but she also managed the house, did the gardening and mowed the lawn. After a day of teaching she would stay up at night making meals for the following day, everything from scratch. She even made many of our clothes. That is, until one day, at the age of eleven I went to school in a beautiful homemade denim outfit with designs on the cuffs. That day I came home and begged her to stop making my clothes. I learned to be an overachiever from my mom—and I also learned to stay away from sewing machines.

My mom loved us, but she was not the doting mom, rather she was busy and efficient. I remember one winter day Mom told my brother and me that she would take us swimming at the local pool, so we were both very excited. Well, a massive snowstorm came along. But because her children really wanted to go swimming and she had promised to take us, what did she do that evening but pile us into her red Beetle car and drive to the pool, very carefully, through the wild blowing snow. If you say you're going to do something, then do it and don't make excuses, even if there is a blizzard in your way. I think being a single parent much of the time made my mom a very determined woman.

I now see that my parents had an unusually strong relationship. They somehow had an agreement about the division of roles that worked for our family. My mother had a career yet managed most aspects of our home. She took care of the children much of the time as well, but she had the advantage and comfort of being rooted to our community. She also had the security of knowing that my father, although away, was very supportive of her decisions. My father missed us when he was gone, but when he was home, it was all about us as a family. My parents had decided early on that this was how they wanted to live. That was my unique childhood.

I sometimes look back, amazed that my mom could do all that she did. That she could work every day as a teacher, take care of us and run the house, and still manage to keep her hair done and always be dressed to the nines. In her closet, my mother had a row of high heels and a rack of beautiful skirts. As a little girl I loved going into my mom's closet to see the pretty blouses that smelled like the Nina Ricci perfume that she always wore. She was tough, but she was feminine too, and proud. And she was efficient. She didn't have time to be the mom that spent hours making crafts with us on the floor or take us for long afternoons in the park. We were shooed out of the house when we were old enough to ride our bikes, and we were told to amuse ourselves until mealtime.

So I would go off in the morning on my bicycle and not get home until lunch. Most of the neighborhood kids were like this, we were given a sense of freedom to explore. Our parents understood the importance of this experience, and they believed that lessons were best learned out in the world. If we made mistakes, they trusted we would learn from them, and do better next time.

But let's face it, sometimes we do and sometimes we don't. My brother and I were walking home one biting winter day, one of those days when everything is gray and white and frozen over. When we got to our house, my brother, two years older than me and who liked to challenge me, said, "Dare you to put your tongue there," pointing with a mitten-covered finger to the black cast iron railings along the sides of the steps. I thought it sounded like a silly dare and an easy thing to do. So I stuck my whole six-year-old tongue out and applied it to the metal. I felt the fierce pain immediately. My tongue had stuck to the frozen railing and I was trapped there, bent over it, attached by my tongue, horrified. Finally, I had to rip my tongue away. Of course it hurt like crazy and there was blood everywhere, but I never did that again.

Later, my father said to me, "Most kids, when they are dared to do something, don't do it. But not you—you have to put your whole self into it." That was it. When I went at things, I went at them wholeheartedly. I couldn't help it. And even though sometimes it got me into trouble, it was just the way I was.

Growing up, I was never made to feel I should be afraid to do things. I wasn't raised with gender stereotypes, but I was expected to listen up and behave. I'm sure there were times when my parents shook their heads and wondered what I would end up like; their only daughter, who seemed intent on cutting her own trail. I was always out on my bicycle dealing with the world in my own way, taking on dares and rarely shying away from challenges. I guess I pretty much always believed I could face the consequences of my actions. Maybe that was tempting fate a little though.

It seemed back then that there wasn't a day that didn't go by without someone crossing my path. There were the usual number of kids who liked to pick a fight for no apparent reason. There was one boy, Rodney Sanders—he didn't like me and I didn't like him. Who knows why. We were both about eight years old. One day out on our bikes, he called out, "Gilliguts, who's chicken?" If you wanted to get my hackles up, all you had to do was call me *that* name. I was on my little gold bicycle, riding barefoot as usual. I was not one to turn down a dare, especially from stinky little Rodney Sanders. So I shouted, "Yeah, Sanders, you're the chicken!" He had turned his bike around and was about a block from me, but even at that distance, I could see his freckled face getting all red as he yelled back, "You are!" We stared at each other a minute. I wasn't going to back down. I knew that. So, glaring at each other, off we went full tilt and smashed our bikes head on. We landed on the ground in a heap of mangled bikes, me gripping a bleeding foot that had slipped from the pedal.

I hobbled home and as my mom bandaged me up, even the pain didn't override the pride I felt for standing my ground. I sat there in high spirits because I knew if I could match chicken with bully Rodney Sanders, there was nothing that I couldn't do.

But sometimes, I actually liked to play with dolls and kitchen sets and make tea parties. Dad often brought us gifts when he returned and loved to hear the squeals of delight as he opened up his luggage with us hovering over his shoulder. I remember one time he came home with a beautiful doll's pram. He must have had visions of his blond-headed daughter walking her dollies up and down the street. At that time, we had a rabbit, Buttons, which we kept in a cage in the back yard. When I saw the pram, I had an idea. I took that beautiful doll pram and set out to the backyard. Buttons was there in the corner of the cage, along with some lettuce leaves, dozing or maybe just trying to stay out of reach of busy little girls with suspicious intentions. Reaching way inside, I was able to scoop him out of the cage and plop him into the pram. Smart rabbit kept trying to jump out, but I held him tight. I was sure I could persuade him to like the pram, and that we would have a fine time, so I drove my new pram with one hand on the handle and the other hand clutching the rabbit's ears, talking to him the whole time. Of course, Buttons got away. My dad spent the rest of the morning chasing the rabbit through the neighborhood, cursing like crazy at it, me and the situation.

That's the kind of daughter the parents of GirlPreneurs often need to put up with. Daughters who are not afraid to take a challenge even if they might wind up with some scraped knees.

GirlPreneurs do the unexpected and we cut our own trails.

Popularity is Overrated

In Grade 4, I was the tallest in my class, and when you're the tallest kid in class it can seem like everything else about you stands out too. Your arms reach the highest. Your feet look the longest. Even my name sounded tall. F-i-o-n-a. And my last name, Gilligan, well, enough said. I had never been popular, but in Grade 4, I set out to change that. I was going to be popular. I was going to fit in, come rain or shine. So I watched and waited for the right opportunity and knew I would recognize it when it came along.

In early November, my chance struck. In Miss Watson's class, our crowning achievements were to be our mid-year presentations. We'd been instructed to start thinking about our topics. I knew this could be my opportunity to shift the wind of popularity in my direction, and I knew how I was going to do it. Girls loved dolls. I was going to organize a doll competition and we would all have a chance to share our stories about our best things. I could foresee the mountains of birthday invitations coming my way.

Confessions of a GirlPRENEUR | 13

The week of the presentations arrived. There was excitement in the air. Days earlier I had sent out notes to all my classmates inviting them to bring their dolls and figurines to school on the day of my presentation. My surprise was going to be that everyone was going to win a prize regardless of how ugly or worn their toy was. In Fiona's Doll Show we were all going to win. And that win was going to be a bag of candy. I had divvied out enough from various sources, namely my house and my grandmother's, and had counted out enough little bags. I stashed it all in a box that said, "Presentation." How I managed to get away with taking bags of candy still puzzles me. The big day arrived, and enterprising me was ready for the applause.

The problem, I didn't realize, was that kids didn't like having their toys ranked and rated. Katie didn't want her Shirley doll judged against Susie's Veronica doll and that against Jason's new GI Joe. Kids clutched their prized possessions, fights broke out, tears and snot galore. The show ended up causing all kinds of tension and friction in the class. It was a disaster. Instead of everyone liking me, they all gave me the stink eye; the air full of ruffled feathers, just like that old crow. And I never got a chance to hand out the candy, which in hindsight, might have quickly remedied the situation.

Even though I'd pictured everyone a winner, and me at the center of the winning crowd, Grade

4 didn't quite live up to my expectations. In June, as we were getting ready for summer break, I was still the tallest in the class. I still had to wait my turn for the swirly swings even when I just wanted to jump in front of the line. Reading, writing, arithmetic, it was all a bit boring I found, so I was often coming up with my own solutions to problems. I was aware that I was different, but I could never really pinpoint why. Nothing had really changed.

If I was in trouble, it was usually for talking too much, talking out of turn, or just generally not following the rules. I was naughty enough to be normal. Well, maybe a bit more naughty than normal, but I had good marks and the teachers liked me. I also had a deep-rooted sense of independence that was becoming more and more obvious. I often felt bored and disengaged, and because of this, I had to make up my own fun. My classmates wanted to follow instructions and move on to recess, whereas I wanted to implement a charting system for our seating assignments or find out what percentage of students would like more gym time.

Only outside my house did I ever get the message that girls shouldn't do all the same things boys do; that girls didn't get into scrapes, make charting systems, have races or arm wrestling contests, or speak boldly. My parents raised my brother and me in the same way. We both had to help with the dishes. We were both given bikes and balls and pogo sticks and told to go out and do our best.

Confessions of a GirlPRENEUR | 15

I was determined to be a pogo champ. My neighbor Brady McFlint was my nemesis. He was always calling me a sissy and saying girls were "stupid ." Brady had a pogo stick too. Rumor had it that he'd gotten over 1,000 pogo hops, which was huge. I decided the best way to get back at him was to beat him at his own game. I felt I had a decent chance because I took my pogo stick everywhere. I didn't walk, I pogoed. One day when all the kids were outside, I brought out my stick and challenged Brady to a contest. The kids counted. I hopped. And hopped. And hopped. I didn't make it to 1,000 but I came very close - in the 900's.

That afternoon, I went home with blood blisters. My mom looked at my hands and sighed. By now she knew—what else could she expect from her daughter? I realized early on that I had to be tough to hang in there. I also had to be good at things. I learned some valuable GirlPreneur skills as a rough-and-tumble kid. It wasn't about winning, 'cause I didn't exactly care about that, it was that I learned to get out there and do things. I learned to not be afraid to put myself in the game.

The rest of elementary school would fly by in that same vein. I eventually let go the idea of becoming "popular." In my own way, I started to transfer that awareness of being different and not really fitting in into an empathy for the underdog. In middle school there was an Asian kid named Darren who lived on my street. After school when we were all walking home, the other kids—the bullies—would tease him and call him awful names. He was the only Asian kid in our school, and because of this difference in those days, he didn't seem to have any friends. He was always walking home by himself.

One day, I ran and caught up with Darren. We didn't talk about much except things like whose classes we were in. After that, I started catching up to Darren regularly or I'd notice that he'd be waiting for me, though never obviously. That walk home became a symbol for me that seeking out a certain kind of popularity was not who I was. I didn't even like the popular kids nearly as much as I liked my new friend Darren. I tried to remember that what I thought about myself was more important than what others thought about me.

There was a boy on my street, Gary Crump, a big kid and a real bully. One day, I was his target. He was making fun of me because I had walked home with Darren. I used words to try to make him stop, but he didn't. So when he got into my face, I hauled back and punched him hard. It felt great—even though a second later he punched me right back. We had a big kerfuffle and both ended up a little battle scarred, but I had stood up for myself and my friend, and Gary never bothered us again.

Maybe that's why I stood apart a little. Because the kids noticed when a girl gave the bully boy a taste of his own medicine. From a young age, I had learned to follow my instincts about people. I learned that watching and listening can tell you a lot. I saw the smirks on the gossipy girls' faces, heard the boasts from the insecure kids, felt the stares of girls who didn't happen to share my taste in boy's shorts and grass-stained T-shirts. Life can sometimes be mean at the same time that it appears to be sunny.

Bullies! We all remember them and have had to deal with them. Kids that loved lording over other unsuspecting kids. It was easy to spot in the younger years. Boy bullies threw insults or started fights. But later, it was more subtle when I started to encounter girl bullies. Girls can have their own brand of bullying. It can be bullying by exclusion or innuendo. Girl bullies, like Miss Goody Two Shoes, in all her self-righteous glory, is just a bully in a sweater set. Miss Goody Shoes didn't invite me to her birthday party, but made sure that she mentioned her party in front of me as many times as humanly possible.

Girls also bully by forming cliques and not accepting those with differences. I never understood this. I always believed the more the merrier, and the more variety the better. I even hated picking kids for my birthday parties because I wanted everyone to come. I never wanted to exclude anyone. I'm not saying I was perfect, I just didn't like to hurt people's feelings and I knew full well what not getting invited felt like.

Even if I was never going to win the popularity contest, I at least discovered that I had the gift of gab and the ability to talk my way into and out of most things. On Fridays I would have a brown bag lunch. There would almost always be a peanut butter sandwich, a candy bar and a can of pop. My lunches had a good reputation. As soon as I opened my bag, someone would say, "Oh, you got a candy bar again. Want to trade for my chips?" They should have known that a candy bar had much greater value in the lunchroom economy than a bag of chips. "Forget it," I would respond. "But…if you want to give me the chips *and* something else, then maybe I'll trade." Before I knew it, I'd have two or more things for that one candy bar and all parties still felt like they'd gotten a deal.

Some might call it persuasion. As a Brownie, prancing up to the door with my wagon full of boxes determined to be the one who sold the most, I could talk until magically there were no more boxes in my wagon.

In my own way, that is how I became "popular." It was by doing what came naturally to me, which was speaking up and speaking out of turn, interrupting conversations, taking action and always wanting everyone to be involved. If popularity is being well known for something, then by the end of middle school, I had definitely established my own brand of being popular.

Confessions of a GirlPRENEUR | 19

Today, when I speak to groups of girls and women I recognize that same spunk. Your entrepreneurial fire is alive in your eyes and your gift of gab. Your ability to become a successful entrepreneur is real if you trust and believe in yourself.

Go get in the game! Don't wait to be invited. There is never a perfect time. Know that you can do it. Look back on your childhood, when you were a bossy little girl and got things done. And if you weren't a bossy little girl? It doesn't matter! It is never too late to tap into that go-getter spirit. GirlPreneurs get things done.

The Beauty of Brevity

When my brother and I were kids, my dad was away for long periods of time, sometimes for months. As a Canadian Air Force pilot he was stationed at various locations throughout his career. I loved seeing him in his uniform; he looked so important. I remember one night—it must have been a special state occasion—when Dad had to fly the plane carrying the Canadian Prime Minister. My mom took us to the airport. The Prime Minister's wife was there with her kids and their security detail. She was very nice; she talked to me and asked my name. The plane arrived and they put down the carpet for the Prime Minister. After he and the other passengers were out, there stood my dad in his gray full-body flight uniform. At that moment, he was my super hero, my idol. I remember that moment like it was yesterday.

In the latter part of my childhood, Dad was stationed at a base three hours from home. He lived and worked at the base during the week and came home on weekends. Earlier on, my mother had decided she did not want to move her children around every few years, so we had a weekend father for a good part of my childhood.

Friday night my brother and I would sit by the window watching and waiting for his car to pull into the driveway. Then there he would be, walking in the door, tall and handsome, throwing his arms around us. He was a warm, giving type of guy, with big blue eyes and a great laugh. He really liked to laugh. We'd have a big dinner. But we didn't race away from the table the minute we had gobbled down our food. My brother and I would stay and listen to my mom and dad and grandmother while they discussed all kinds of topics. My mom and dad especially liked politics. Then we'd all sit in the family room together and watch sitcoms. This was our Friday night ritual.

Saturday we'd be out the door early, my brother, my dad, and me. In the winter months, we'd be on the ski hill by 9:00 am and would ski all day. Dad would carry containers of hot chocolate he had made himself. We'd get lunch in the chalet. Mom had her Saturday rituals—Loretta's for bread and boxes of pastries for Saturday night, the Glebe Meat Market for meat and gossip, Badalli's for fruits and vegetables. When Dad was home we led a very traditional family life.

Some Saturday nights, Dad would take Mom out to the Officer's Mess. Mom would have her hair done. They'd come downstairs all dressed up, Mom wearing perfume, Dad in his formal uniform. They loved to spend evenings together eating, drinking and dancing.

On Saturdays when we didn't ski, Dad would fix things around the house or work on his car. In fact, there was someone else in their marriage: the Volvo. Dad could build stuff, repair stuff and install stuff. When the oil embargo hit in the 70's and the government created incentives for energy conservation, my dad did the research and figured out how to build and install solar panels. We were the first ones on our block to have solar panels—by several decades. Dad was an environmentalist, though he wouldn't have used that word. This passion came from a combination of frugality and an interest in innovation.

Thanks to his training, he was very driven by metrics. Being a pilot, he was always charting. We both loved to run, and he showed me how to chart my route and keep track of my time. It took me a while to get better, but he showed me how to break down the challenge into doable parts, how to take incremental steps to achieve big goals.

During high school, when my homework was piled high on my desk and I was feeling overwhelmed, I'd remember Dad's strategies. I'd say to myself, *Ok, I'm going to break it down into bite-sized pieces. I'm going to do 20 minutes of geography then*

Confessions of a GirlPRENEUR | 23

20 minutes of math and suddenly it didn't seem so daunting anymore. Later, when I was in business, I would apply these same approaches to planning and goal setting.

As I've said, Dad was a keen runner. If the evening was nice, he'd be out the door with his trainers on. He'd start off in the driveway by taking his heart rate, set a stop watch and go. If I joined him, he'd keep track of our pace at all the main intersections. Sometimes he'd arrive home after a run and say, "Ah, two minutes over…" sounding disappointed, but a minute later he'd be laughing at something.

Dad taught me that in life you are mostly competing against yourself. It is usually you standing in your way more than anyone or anything else. Whether the challenge was running or homework, you had to maintain a sense of humour when you were not at your best. That was my dad's artistry. He understood that we must sometimes overcome our own selves, and that doing well requires both discipline and grace. Whether you win or lose is ultimately up to you.

On Sundays we'd go to church. But my father liked a short and sweet service. Like many in his generation, he had an ambivalent relationship with the church. He was a very strategic Catholic. We had to change churches several times before he found a priest who understood the beauty of brevity. On those other occasions when we found ourselves two hours into the sermon, Dad would doze off or fidget in his seat or, worse, he would start to quietly mutter. My brother and I would be snickering while my grandmother, who was deaf, would look over at him and say, "What's that, Connor?" There was my sweet grandmother with her rosary beads while her son grumbled away under his breath.

Dad created special traditions. Like birthdays. In our house, if it was your birthday, you gave small presents to everyone else. He liked to give; he wasn't comfortable getting things from others.

Some Saturday mornings when I was small, Dad would take me to the local smoke shop in the Glebe. It was the unofficial hangout for the Irishmen in the neighborhood. I'd be on Dad's hip listening to the men talk politics, war, sports and gossip. Then Dad would buy the newspaper for his mother and we'd go home to see what everyone else was up to.

Sometimes when the day was clear and there wasn't anything around that needed prompt fixing, Dad would say, "Let's go and fly a plane." He'd rent a two-seater Cessna. As a pilot, he followed a strict protocol of checks and cross checks. It took a long time to safety check the whole aircraft, but finally we'd taxi off, talking with the local air traffic control tower with our headsets on. We'd fly over

Confessions of a GirlPRENEUR | 25

the neighbourhood, right over our house and my school. He would have one control and I would have the other one. We had great conversations up there in the air. That's where he seemed the most relaxed.

I remember that he offered to teach me to fly. Imagine having a father who wanted to teach his daughter to fly! I loved the fact that he made me that offer. I wish I had taken him up on it.

The Game

Like all teen girls, I crossed over the invisible bridge from childhood into adolescence. In high school, I made good grades, played tennis and had a job at a daycare in the summer months. We were a typical middle-class family with parents raising us to be educated and find well-paying jobs. From the outside it probably looked like the perfect life, and in many ways it was. But a family can only bring a girl so far.

Even though my family never set up gender obstacles, in the real world outside my home, the messages were everywhere; there was an undercurrent, a pervasive subtext to everything. There was pressure to be good and look good. The world was telling the teen girl that fitting in was better than standing out. In fact, standing out might not only be considered bad taste, but could also isolate you from your peers.

Like many girls, in those teen years I started to feel boxed in. I felt the pressure to behave appropriately: no more cursing for the fun of it,

Confessions of a GirlPRENEUR | 27

sit with your legs crossed, style your hair every day, have manners. Those were the overt messages that we were getting. It was confusing and a bit of a struggle to understand this game of becoming a teenage girl. Putting pretty ahead of smart, being demure instead of assertive. What was going on? Many girls got caught in this game to fit in, at a time when we were already off-kilter as a result of being in the thick of adolescence.

As girls, we have vivid memories of the impact of our changing bodies and emotions. It became apparent that people were changing their attitudes toward us, be it friends, family, teachers or neighbors. We were becoming young women, even if in many ways we were still children. Becoming a teenager meant a lot of the naiveté we'd had as girls bucking roles was now starting to disappear. We were now expected to behave in certain ways, even if those ways didn't always come naturally. One day you're a free-spirited girl who doesn't think things through—you are living in the moment, having fun, being curious, exploring around you—and the next thing you know, rules appear. Rules and judgments that govern us. I couldn't just talk out of turn anymore.

It didn't happen all at once, of course. It crept up on us by degrees. I remember one event in particular. It was after school and a lot of the kids were roaming around the front yards, playing a tag game called British bulldog. A version of this game had been going on for years, and whatever group of kids happened to be outside after school would play. There I was in my knee socks and shorts, alongside the neighborhood boys. I was reaching out to try to tag somebody who had gotten just out of my reach as several others kids weaved around us, and as I dipped back, I caught someone's sleeve and we all fell into a pile. Others rushed over and piled on top of us. One of the neighborhood moms looked over to see a 13-year-old girl tangled up on the lawn with a pack of boys, flushed and grass-stained. She gave me a disapproving look and went back inside. In that moment, I got the message that falling into a pile of British bulldoggers was not an appropriate thing to be doing. I went inside my house, ashamed but not knowing exactly why.

It might sound like a very small thing, but I never played that game again. It just never felt right. That might have been the first moment I felt ashamed to be a girl, the first time I got the mysterious sense that, although I had done nothing wrong, I was still somehow guilty. The boys did not get those looks.

But as girls, we did. And more, we were told to change. One sweltering hot June day in Junior High, as I was walking down the hall to class, Mr. Hardy stopped me and pulled me aside, "Does your mom know you're wearing that?" he asked. I looked down at my tank top and wasn't sure if it was

Confessions of a GirlPRENEUR | 29

that or my jeans he was referring to. "Yes, sir, she does," I said. "I don't think so," he replied, "You can't wear a tank top to class." "I had a shirt, but it's so hot, I took it off," I explained. He told me to go get my shirt and cover up. As I went into class, I looked at all the guys who were wearing their tank top shirts and knew that they hadn't been advised to cover up. I was angry but I said nothing.

Really, what were my choices? I had tried to make my case, but I was told to comply. But where does a girl go with this unfairness, this anger? As girls, many choose to ignore the inequity as a coming of age phenomena. Yet others choose to compensate and react by provoking, be it in their looks, behavior, or what have you. For me, I dealt with it through a combination of all of the above, but to be sure, sports and friends became pivotal in my life.

The pressure to act a certain way is counterintuitive to the warriors that girls really are: artists, athletes, scientists—and GirlPreneurs. It is hard work being a teen girl, often paddling against strong currents, trying to hold on to who we are. A passion for something and a great gaggle of like-minded friends can keep a girl confident and sure of herself as she transitions into adulthood. I made it through high school by playing tennis, skiing hard, and relying on a few close friends.

Drifting

When I graduated from high school with honors, I was accepted into all the good universities. It was rewarding to see the letters arrive in their official-looking envelopes, but I hadn't given much thought to where I wanted to go. There was no particular university that I felt destined to attend. I'd set my sights on pursuing a degree in psychology. Even in those early years, I knew that I wanted to work helping people.

Although I had a strong idea of what I wanted to study, in many ways I had peaked in high school and I was academically exhausted. Yet, I felt I should be doing what all my friends were doing, enrolling right away in University and starting the march towards a serious career. Most of them were going away to the best schools.

In hindsight, I probably would have benefited from taking a year off. Maybe I should have worked in retail, gotten a restaurant job or backpacked around Europe before settling down to study. Sometimes you simply need to admit that taking

Confessions of a GirlPRENEUR | 31

pauses in life can be recharging. Instead, I started university that fall, but it quickly became clear that I just wasn't ready.

That first year I was very lost. The bottom fell out for me. I started failing many of my courses and I didn't know whether I was coming or going. Sometimes I went to the student pub for lunch and ended up not leaving until two in the morning, playing endless games of backgammon and pool. I was not motivated to go to class or to worry about exams. One day would blend into the next. At the end of the year, I was an academic train wreck. For the first time in my life, I was failing.

It got worse from there. I decided to move out of my parents' house and into an apartment downtown with some acquaintances who were in a hurry to find a roommate. The place was a dirt-cheap three-bedroom. It was a dump, but we thought we were living the dream! Parties, drinking and dating. I had no focus, no clarity and no ambition, but I was having the time of my life, not worrying about a thing! For the first time in my life, I took the pressure off myself to be a super-achiever.

That was my first year of university. My parents never knew I was failing. But my days of partying slipped into days of feeling lost and disengaged. I started to not know what I was doing with my life. I had the usual dinners every week with my family. I still went to all the family gatherings and managed to appear as if everything was peachy keen. I didn't want to worry them. My parents were paying for my university expenses while assuming that everything was going well.

But nothing could have been further from the truth. Eventually, I was summoned by the dean and warned that unless my marks improved I would be expelled from the B.A. Honours program to which I had been admitted as a result of my high school academic record. I walked out of the dean's office, visualizing the huge mountain I had to climb after wasting a full year. Now I had to make up for that time. The pressure was suffocating, but at the same time it provided the catalyst I needed to turn my life around.

Failing was my wakeup call. I didn't overthink it, I just put an action plan in place. Within a few months, I had moved out of the squalid dump. My instincts kicked in and I moved in with two girls who liked a clean house. We still had fun, but I started to think about things differently. After a year of goofing off, I realized that I didn't want to be a nobody. I wanted to be a somebody, and that was going to require hard work, discipline, and a solid plan. I also had to quit a smoking habit I had acquired after high school and get back into physical condition. That year of screwing up had been a freeing experience, but overall it had left me feeling dull, anxious and dissatisfied.

Confessions of a GirlPRENEUR | 33

I was ready to get it together. I started going to classes again and was spending my Saturday nights in the library instead of the pub. I enrolled in summer school courses to make up my lost credits and made a schedule for myself. I was going to graduate and I was going to stay in the B.A. Honours program.

By the end of the second year of university, I had turned things around. I was pulling in A's and B's. I was doing well. I had turned the failure into a challenge. My father had encouraged me to get out there and do things. I remembered those runs we went on together that gave me such an amazing feeling of accomplishment. Once you've had that feeling you can tap into it, and eventually doing the work becomes its own reward.

I tapped into the lessons of my childhood, applied them to a problem to overcome it. In July of 1988, I finished my B.A. in psychology and graduated with Honours. I got a summer job waiting tables until I could find a permanent position in my field.

One smoldering hot afternoon in July, after a shift at the restaurant, I was walking home. I remember what a beautiful summer day it was, but little did I know that within minutes, my life and that of my family would change fundamentally and forever.

Just as I opened the door to my apartment, I heard the phone ringing. I quickly ran to answer it and on the other end was the Parish Priest. Immediately, I knew that something was wrong when he asked if he could come over to speak with me. He never called, and in fact, I barely knew him or him me. My heart started to race and I got that awful feeling that something bad had happened but I didn't know what. I thought of my brother working in Africa, my Mom who had not been well, but never in my life did I imagine that it was my father.

Fifteen minutes later, sitting on my couch next to the family priest, he told me that my Dad had died suddenly while working in Saudi Arabia. Everything else he said afterwards was lost in a fog of shock. Life stood completely still.

That was the day that my life fundamentally changed forever. My hero, my father, was dead.

Up in the Air

The Irish love a party, even if it's to bury a loved one. So we had a two-week Irish wake and burial. By the end, I was exhausted. I don't know how my mother made it through. Maybe it was all of the people who swarmed around us and helped every step of the way, then again, maybe that made it more difficult. But it was at the reception at our house, surrounded by all the Air Force personnel who attended along with our extended Irish family, that I got the idea that would help me deal with it all.

I was going to fly. I was going to join the airlines. I was going to fly—I suddenly knew that.

A month later I did a couple of interviews and within six weeks, I was in flight school. I was following my dad's mottos: "Just start. Get your boots on. Get in the game." In this case, I was getting into my blue flight attendant's uniform because I was hired by a local airline, doing turn-around flights from Iqaluit to Ottawa. One half of the plane was passengers, the other half was cargo. I was hired as a flight attendant, but I was really cargo crew as well. Some girls would have balked at that, but I liked it. It was exhausting and it was adventurous, even if I did have to heave 50 pound boxes of dry goods. I mean we're talking about airplanes flying to the North landing beside the Arctic Ocean in whiteout conditions and -40 degree Celsius temperatures. I must have been in a state of denial, but I found it exhilarating.

Part of me needed this. In the air, I'd remember all the times I flew above Ottawa perched beside my dad, how we'd shared so many conversations while soaring over the world below. Sometimes I would actually feel we were together again. I suppose that is why I decided to join the airlines in the first place, to try to recreate that time. I wanted to be with him, not forget him. Sometimes I would ask the pilots, "Did you ever know Connor Gilligan?" Since a lot of the DC-10s were flown by ex-Canadian Air Force pilots, it was possible that they could have worked together. I knew Dad would have loved seeing me in my flight attendant uniform at the loading door of a passenger jet, going over the evacuation procedures before take-off.

If I had meant to escape by joining the airlines, it was working. The schedule and the conditions were demanding. After six months of working with the local airline, I decided to raise the bar. I set my sights on working for what I considered to be a

Confessions of a GirlPRENEUR | 37

more sophisticated outfit. I got hired by WardAir, the best airline around, and was posted to Toronto. I took the job immediately even though it meant moving—in fact, this was exactly why I took the job.

When a group of people are in a capsule flying 40,000 feet above the earth, a few are bound to be petrified. When we were loading one summer evening for a flight from Toronto to London, England, one of the airline agents had warned us there was a passenger who was afraid of flying. He was in one of the fear-of-flight management programs offered at the time and they had identified him to the staff. As the man boarded we could see he was sweaty and nervous.

The plane was full with 460 passengers and at takeoff I was facing the passengers, smiling as we always did. As the plane began to move down the runway, engines powering up, I could see the man's eyes bulging like a bug, staring at me from 10 rows away. The plane's nose started to lift off, the force of it pushing the passengers back in their seats, the galley shaking. All of a sudden the man threw off his seat belt, jumped up and started screaming, "Let me off!" As he ran down the aisle, the male stewards tackled him. He was yelling, "You're holding me against my rights!" By this time all the passengers were agitated. The man then went from screaming to sobbing as he was taken back to his seat, and a doctor that happened to be on the flight gave him something to calm him down. I probably learned more about human behaviour working as a flight attendant on a Boeing 747 than I ever would in graduate school.

Moving to Toronto had been an important stepping stone on the path to accepting my dad's death. It was important for me to continue to feel a connection to him, but I also knew I had to move forward and try to turn adversity into something positive. I had taken the job with the airlines to connect to my dad, but maybe it was time to think about what I really wanted to do after that. I wanted to make a difference. I wanted to help people. That was still clear to me.

At first I felt lonely in Toronto, so I decided that when I wasn't scheduled to fly, I would get involved by volunteering with non-profit organizations that supported women, and I met tons of new people who were impassioned by these causes. It was a funny life, one part high heels and a so-called glamorous lifestyle, the other part Birkenstocks and activism!

After one more year of flying, I decided it was time to move on. I had been volunteering for over a year, and becoming a social worker was what I'd set my sights on. The people I was meeting and becoming friends with, the ones who seemed genuinely passionate, were all social workers.

Confessions of a GirlPRENEUR | 39

So I left WardAir and moved back to Ottawa. I talked to the social workers in Toronto and Ottawa and realized that if I wanted a job in the social work field I would need to get a master's degree. I was told specifically to try for the Master of Social Work (MSW) program at Carleton University, which was a one of a kind program. It was extremely hard to get into this program; there were over 900 applicants and only 80 openings. So I applied a serious strategy that began with calling the program coordinator, who I quickly realized was the gatekeeper for new applicants. I wanted her to know my name and to realize how dedicated I was and how badly I wanted to be accepted into the program.

It was a tough sell. I had to educate the graduate committee that my time as a flight attendant gave me abundant experience dealing with human behaviour and personality and complemented my degree in psychology. I asked them point blank if they had any idea what it was like to be a flight attendant. I explained that the glamour ends when you get on the airplane and you are focused on safety and human dynamics. Sometimes you are dealing with some people in their worst state; maybe tired, scared, drunk or panicky. I'd witnessed and intervened with it all. After several detailed stories of flight experiences, the committee said, "Go ahead and submit your application."

The day I was accepted into the program, was one of the happiest of my life. Since it was such a

40 | Fiona Gilligan with Kendall McQueen

reputable program, the student body was diverse; there were students from everywhere. And for the next two years while I studied, I also became a community activist for women's rights. I was fighting for the underdogs and I'd never worked so hard in my life. It was fantastic!

I finished my master's in social work and got a job quickly after graduation, working for a child welfare organization. It was a full-time and well-paid job and I grabbed it because after being in university a total of six years, I was up to my eyeballs in student debt. I knew that I needed a job that offered security and stability. I was not only tired of living like a student, but knew I had to rid myself of that debt load. I told myself it wasn't the perfect job, but it was a paycheck and I was lucky to have one.

Still, this new job was heavily administrative and I wanted something more gritty and front-line. I wanted to get in front of people and be working with them. After all that hard work and resourcefulness, I was working a job that didn't feel right, but I had to bide my time. I knew myself well enough to know that if it didn't feel right, it wasn't right. Another change was imminent.

This is a common theme for the GirlPreneur, seeking new challenges immediately after conquering the previous one, setting new goals the instant a milestone has been passed. It can seem like restlessness or indecisiveness, but in retrospect it is often a sign that we are meant for work where we set the rules rather than trying to fit into a role that has been defined by somebody else.

Sitting on a Rock

I was never in the habit of reading the careers section of the newspaper, but ten months later on a Saturday morning I happened to find myself bored and doing exactly that. My attention was caught by an ad—for a social worker at a lead trauma hospital. The posting piqued my interest because it was gritty frontline crisis work and I knew I had to apply.

I did and I got called in for an interview the following week. I had the right background and personality. But there was a catch: the job was only part-time and I needed a full-time salary. It seemed foolish to leave a full-time salaried position with benefits. The following Thursday, when the hospital called and offered me the social work job, I told them I would let them know the next Monday. That Saturday, I went with my family to a friend's house for dinner out on the lakeshore.

It was a beautiful, hot afternoon. I was sitting on a rock by the lake while I told my mom and brother I had been offered a part-time job in the

Confessions of a GirlPRENEUR | 43

emergency department at the hospital. I told them I didn't know what I should do. My brother, who has always been a logical thinker and a good friend to me, listened to me going on about the pros and cons. Then, with clear words of encouragement, he just said, "Fiona, it sounds like a great job for you."

Little did I know that sitting on a rock by a lake that afternoon, I was about to make a decision that would change the trajectory of my life. I was about to discover my calling and start my career as a trauma therapist that would eventually lead me down the path to GirlPreneurship. As I looked out at the lake spreading before me on that long summer day, I decided that I would risk it. Even though I had only ten months ago started my first real job, I knew that working as part of a trauma team was what I was meant to do. It just felt right.

So I took the job and started two weeks later.

From the moment I walked into the controlled chaos that is a busy emergency department—the antiseptic smell, the harsh lighting, the rushed-yet-calm non-stop activity of the staff—I knew I had made the right decision. I was immediately called into action, using my crisis training and experience to help the team deal with victims and their families. Even though it was a place full of tragedy, the environment was incredibly positive.

Working in emergency as a trauma counselor for three years gave me the chance to witness the power of the human spirit and its resilience in the midst of incredible suffering. Day-in and day-out through critical circumstances, our patients made me realize what matters most in life. When people are hurt or dying, they never talk about how they should have worked harder or made more money. They simply want to be surrounded by the people they love. They want their lives to have stood for something meaningful.

The emergency department would get a call from the paramedic dispatch saying that an ambulance was on its way and provide the details of what had occurred. The minute we received the call, the emergency team would get gloved up and ready, observation beds would be prepared and everyone on the trauma team would be notified. I would feel my adrenaline surge as I got ready to respond, to gather information for the medical team and to work with the victims and their families. Then the ambulance would whip in, doors flying open, and the paramedics would be running down the hall while doing chest compressions or whatever else was necessary to keep the patient alive.

Alongside the team, I dealt with patients and family members who had been called to the hospital after critical and life-threatening events. I sat outside operating rooms and beside hospital beds. I was there when doctors had to tell people that a

Confessions of a GirlPRENEUR | 45

loved one was tragically injured or dead. The job was multi-disciplinary, fast-paced and gritty. I was dealing with many different types of cases; I was helping people and it felt like home.

Sometimes it can take a while to figure out what we want to do. My path to becoming a trauma worker had not been clear or straight. We have to learn what we are good at, the conditions in which we work best, what types of people we work well with, and most importantly trust our instinct to guide us in the right direction. It is through putting ourselves out there and trying new experiences that we gain a sense of who we are and what we want.

Forging our own path as GirlPreneurs and remaining open to possibilities will allow us to see opportunities when they arise and to have the courage to seize them.

Career Code-Blue

Working with people in their time of crisis within the complex administrative and care delivery structure of a hospital, I found I had many ideas about how to improve the system. At the hospital, social workers in the emergency department worked with emergency medical services (EMS)—doctors, nurses and community partners—as part of the trauma response team. The program had received a grant from the province, so there was a budget. I discovered that our jobs weren't just about providing clinical services, we also needed to show that we could keep the program and its consequent funding rolling.

Doctors and nurses focused on the patients' physical healing. The social workers were there to help their emotional and psycho-social healing. The medical staff were often too busy to identify or assess these needs or refer patients to us. So I took the initiative and approached the doctors working the emergency floor to find out if their patients needed social work services.

Confessions of a GirlPRENEUR | 47

Since the program was dependent on the number of referrals we received and the number of people who used our services, I decided the best strategy was to always be present and available. Rather than sitting in my office waiting for someone to call, I moved my work station into the emergency department right alongside the team, perching on a stool or in any space I could find. Staff could see me. (The expression "Out of sight, out of mind" is often only too true.) Taking the initiative led to great referrals. After walking around and asking the team members, "Hey, do you need social work?" we would get nine or ten referrals a night.

This was my introduction to social entrepreneurship.

I became a social entrepreneur by encouraging referrals. Without referrals our program would not survive. I learned to be visible, present and accessible, and because of this the program took off. I'd approach the nurses and the other EMS staff and ask, "How can I help?" Soon I began counseling the staff too. I worked with nurses, police and paramedics—all the people on the front lines of trauma. They sometimes needed to talk about what they had seen and experienced, about being in close proximity to human suffering. I would be standing there and a paramedic would say, "Man, today I picked up body parts..." and I could tell he needed to talk. So he talked and I listened. I was counseling the staff, and many of them started to rely on me.

I had found my calling. Perhaps because I had always understood and empathized with the underdog, perhaps because my father had died suddenly—I'm not quite sure. What I can tell you is that I excelled in my role as a trauma therapist where it was essential to remain calm and caring in the midst of human crisis. And I took immense pride in helping others during times of extraordinary need.

And then came the phone call. At three o'clock one Friday afternoon, I thought it was a bit strange that my boss was meeting me at the department door to personally escort me to his office. Call me slow, but it wasn't until I was seated and introduced to a man from human resources that I twigged to the fact that this might not be a great day for me.

In my three years in the department I had never been sick or late, I'd had perfect performance appraisals and I was well-liked and respected by the trauma team. But a change in management meant that I no longer fit: and with a stroke of a pen and a handshake I was shown the door. I know now that when people get fired they often have no idea it is coming.

Confessions of a GirlPRENEUR | 49

A lot of what was said in that office I've forgotten, or I remember the words as if they were spoken underwater; foggy and confused. I was in shock. There was a short preamble about how much they admired, appreciated and valued my work as a trauma social worker, how much I had contributed to building the emergency department into what it had become. But I was not going to be a part of the program moving forward.

While my boss thanked me for my services, I sat there as the words floated over me: "No longer a position." "Effective immediately." "We'll pack up your office. You don't need to worry about that."

I was being fired! I was then escorted back to the front doors of the hospital. All I can remember is getting into my car, but I had no idea how I got home. How would I tell my mother that I had just been canned from the job I had worked so hard to secure and build? How could they fire me from a job I was so good at and loved so much? I was heartbroken, devastated, and scared.

For several weeks, I was in denial that it had actually happened. In the mornings I would get up and get dressed as if I was going to work. I missed my patients, my colleagues and the hospital environment. I felt that I would never again be so usefully and happily employed.

Although I didn't know it at the time, this was the beginning of my new life as an entrepreneur. Like many other entrepreneurs before and after me, our journey into entrepreneurship often starts with a catalyst.

For me, that catalyst was getting fired.

Getting Launched

After I was let go by the hospital, I found myself with no job and a little bag of severance cash. Of course, I had a big emotional meltdown. I had limited funds to live on until who knew when, so it was a huge shock. I hadn't planned for this curveball that life had thrown me. I'd thought I would have that job forever, or at least until I got married and had my eight kids. (Did I mention my dream in high school was to get married and have eight kids?)

Yet here I was, just myself to feed and care for. My family was great, but they had their own worries. My mom was still dealing with life without Dad. I wasn't about to ask for financial assistance at that point. I had a master's degree, for Pete's sake! The worst thing was that I'd had the cream-of-the-crop job. For a social worker at that time, one of the best jobs to land was a hospital job. It was the most prestigious, best paid, most reliable position you could hope for. So I knew my chances of finding another hospital position in the city after being let go were close to nil.

A close friend had lost her job a few years before I did, so she knew how it felt. She made me come to my senses money-wise. She sat me down. "Ok, Fi, right now, this is what you have. Tally up all your costs: apartment rent, utilities, groceries, miscellaneous like clothing, pharmacy, then travel and social fun money." I sat down and wrote out all my expenses for each month. I gave myself x dollars per month for rent, y for groceries, z for utilities, and so on for auto expenses, entertainment, student loans, etc. Then she said, "Guesstimate it will take you 6 months to start working, to start making any money at all. Take the cash for the month, divvy it up, and that's what you have." I created folders in my wallet. That's how I budgeted.

It was hard. I remember thinking, *you've got to be kidding me.* A few years ago I was flying around the world. Now I was putting $20 a month aside in the travel folder in my wallet. But I knew I had to do it. So that's what I did. On the first of each month, I took money out and divvied it up. If I had $100 left at the end of the month, I'd splurge.

I learned to be clever. We'd go out to dinner, but we'd have drinks at my place beforehand. I learned how to save money by cutting little corners. I learned that I could cut some corners, but that I had to keep some splurges. I could eat beans and tofu instead of meat, but I had to have enough cash to go out Saturday nights and not worry 'too too much' about what dinner cost.

Confessions of a GirlPRENEUR | 53

At this point, it quickly became clear that I needed to try to set up my own business if I was to continue to make ends meet. Even though I knew I didn't want to work at a job that I disliked, I also knew that I didn't have the luxury of time or the savings to be fussy. Besides, the only thing I wanted to do was continue my career as a trauma therapist.

Opening a private counseling practice seemed to be my best option. I had to face it, I was going to have to forge the path ahead, the path to my future, on my own.

The transition into private practice took about six months and a lot of legwork. In the beginning I had no clients. None. But I had my training and I had my experience and I had determination. I invested about $1,000 dollars from the severance savings into start-up costs. I bought a desk, a chair and a couch and outfitted my spare room as an office. I didn't do anything fancy. I was pretty sure that as long as the office was clean and safe and I provided excellent services, the clients wouldn't care that my apartment wasn't some swanky office building downtown. And there was free parking.

That was how I started. Every day I woke up excited and terrified. Both these emotions fuelled those early days of starting out and learning how to manage a business. I always went back to my financial number crunching and asked myself how many clients I had and how many hours I needed for the month. I learned to project, to look down the line and to think ahead. To do that, I started to build my marketing and sales plan around my financial goals. That was my next step.

With my little pink business cards I booted all over Ottawa, meeting people and telling them about my counseling practice. I had packs of cards in my car and I knew all the good bulletin boards in town. I put my cards up, shimmying them into the best spot when no-one was looking. I also offered freebies: I went to community resource centres, wrote little articles in community newspapers—anything I could think of to get the word out that I was in business.

I spent many months going around and introducing myself to people from potential referral sources. I targeted the key groups that would send me referrals that I could turn into clients. I was friendly, open and helpful. I always gave out my information package—a business card and a simple brochure on my services—and I always left with a name and contact information.

Not only that, but I gave many free talks in the community. Doing some business for free is one of the best ways to get the word out about your business. Every day I was marketing and still controlling my costs. Could I do a workshop? Sure!! I would do workshops everywhere. Bereaved families would

Confessions of a GirlPRENEUR | 55

ask if I would speak at their bereavement sessions and I said I would be happy to.

Before I knew it, the phone started ringing with referrals and new clients who wanted to access my services. One person would say she had been referred by her sister-in-law. Another would tell me he had heard me on the radio show or heard my talk at the community centre. My marketing was starting to pay off. I told them about myself and explained the services I was offering, the costs and anything else they wanted to know. I didn't rush the caller; I wanted to gain their trust as a new client. And nine out of ten times, I did. The business started to grow in increments.

My marketing strategy was simple: I had developed my skills over the years and I considered myself to be an excellent trauma therapist. I also gave my clients 10% more in service. I would give them 1 hour and 15 minutes and they could call me between appointments for free, within reason. Sometimes if I felt someone needed help, I would call them to see if they were alright. If someone was in serious trouble, I would see them for free, and I worked incredibly flexible hours. If someone wanted to see me at 5 p.m. on Sunday, I'd schedule a meeting.

I knew other counsellors were charging way more and giving clients less, so I gave my clients more for their money. And this was no gimmick:

I genuinely cared about the clients I was working with.

I was starting to feel that being let go had been a blessing in disguise. Not only was I building a private practice doing what I loved, but I was also doing it on my terms and my income was higher than I had ever imagined. Life was good again; in fact, it was excellent.

When you love what you do, it rarely feels like work. The beauty of being a GirlPreneur is that each day you get to wake up and do what you love.

Peter

While I was still at the emergency department, I had a social work case that would later prove to be instrumental in determining the innovative business structure of the Trauma Management Group. His name was Peter. Peter had been brought to the hospital earlier that year after his car was broadsided as he and two friends were making their way home from a day working on a construction site. Of them all, 21 year-old Peter was the most severely injured, with burns to more than one-third of his body. I met Peter as he lay semi-conscious on a gurney while a staff member shouted out his name to me so that I could begin the family notification process.

I had the task of phoning Peter's mother to let her know that there had been a terrible accident and her son was in serious condition. The hospital needed his medical history, and I asked her to come to the emergency department immediately.

The doctors didn't think Peter was going to live. As I stood at the head of his bed, my job was to keep him calm while the doctors worked to save his life. He drifted in and out of consciousness and I'll never forget the shock that I saw in his eyes. I was briefed on his critical condition and prepared myself for the possibility of having to give the notification to his parents that their son might not survive.

But Peter did not die. He surprised the doctors—first by leaving the operating room alive, and then by making it through the night. It was touch and go for the first 12, 24, and 48 hours. His recovery was slow, but by spring he was out of the hospital and ready to begin what would be a painful two-year physical rehabilitation and a lifelong emotional recovery.

Peter was dealing with an incredible amount of pain. But I was a well-trained, specialized trauma responder by this point. Not only did Peter feel that he had been given a second chance by working with me, but I felt that I had been given another chance to truly help this brave young man.

Peter was in rough shape. He was having day tremors, flashbacks and acute insomnia, and he could barely leave the safety of his home. His mother was thankful that her boy was alive, but the family knew he was never going to be the same again. He still had vivid nightmares about being trapped in a burning vehicle. The counselling process aimed to get Peter to reclaim as much of his life as possible by

Confessions of a GirlPRENEUR | 59

working through his anger at what had happened—anger at the man who had broadsided him, at the miserable blow fate had dealt him and at the physical and psychological wounds that would take years to heal, if they ever would.

Three or four months after I was fired and had set up my private practice, Peter phoned. I was delighted to hear from him because I had never had a chance to say goodbye after I had been let go. He had dropped by the hospital to see me and found out I no longer worked there, so he tracked me down.

When the phone rang and I heard his voice, I was so happy. He said that he felt he still needed therapy and was I available?

Without hesitation I told him, "It would be great to work with you, Peter, but I don't think the hospital would go for it." Since I was in private practice now, my services were no longer covered through the hospital, so clients were required to pay out of pocket. Or so I thought at the time.

"I'm not talking about going to the hospital," he said, "I'll come and see you wherever you are now. My mom can drive me." I told him that yes, I had opened up my own private practice, and I would be honoured to have him as a client, but that I couldn't charge him for my services. It wouldn't feel right after all that he had been through.

"You wouldn't be charging me, Fiona," he explained. "You'd be charging expenses to the insurance company."

"I'd be doing what?" I asked.

"The insurance company. Mom already checked with them. It's all set and they'll pay for all of my counselling."

Peter's mother had done just that. She even had the name and number of a woman at the insurance company who would explain the whole process to me. I contacted her as soon as I got off the phone with Peter. The insurance representative said I could invoice her company directly; Peter and his mother would never see a bill. The company would pay up to $150 an hour for counselling sessions. I couldn't believe it—I was currently charging only $60. I had been prepared to work with Peter for free, so this was astounding news.

That afternoon, I asked many questions. Was there a limit to counselling care? What forms did I need to complete? What did I need to know in order to start working with Peter? The insurance adjuster liked me and was very forthcoming, explaining how the whole accident benefits system worked. She was demonstrating incredible goodwill and obviously wanted Peter to get the help he desperately needed. She was looking for a trauma specialist to refer her clients to, and she told me how happy she was that Peter had found me.

I hung up the phone and sat in silence, trying to take it all in. The insurance coverage of my counselling would allow me to continue working in my field, but in the private sector instead of the public. Moreover, during the time I had been working in the emergency department, when I discharged victims and their families into the community, there were very few trauma counselling services available for them. Families either had to endure lengthy waiting lists or not receive any services at all.

When I had been at the hospital, I had noted this problem in the system. It was a fundamental flaw that had upset us all. The reality was that the victims of traumatic experiences often had to continue to endure the trauma because there was no process in place to serve their needs immediately, and this was when they needed services— immediately.

That night, I could barely sleep. I knew that I was onto something big, very big.

A 24/7 mobile trauma counselling service in the private sector was needed to fill this gap. But nothing like this currently existed: someone would have to build it. This service would help patients like Peter. I also realized that this company would greatly improve the insurance and trauma services industries by creating an alternative billing model where victims and their families did not incur any costs for their counseling.

Within months, I had reached out to other trauma counsellors and asked them to join me so that we could provide more valuable counselling to more people in need by billing existing systems rather than charging the patient. I realized that nothing like this had ever been done before, and I was going to take the leap and start doing it. I was going to be a trailblazer. I was going to start a company.

To determine the validity of the business idea, over the next months I started approaching every professional contact I had—physicians, social workers and EMS staff. I contacted anyone in the industry who would listen to me, telling them I was starting a private trauma counseling company that would not charge victims and their families directly. I asked them if they would use this service, and the answer was an emphatic, "Yes!"

Despite the fact that I had no business experience and I had very limited financial resources to work with, I saw an obvious gap in services for which I could provide a solution—all while capitalizing upon existing funding structures. And most importantly, filling that gap would provide immediate care for victims of trauma and their families.

Confessions of a GirlPRENEUR | 63

The discovery about the insurance funding system was just the beginning. I could build a practice that was funded through various insurance and corporate plans. The business would provide services to and advocate for victims of trauma. Instead of just providing counselling at a one-to-one level in a private practice, I would establish a company that would service all the victims of trauma and their family members who were referred by a wide network of resources in the community and the public and private sectors.

Keep in mind the things you are good at and enjoy doing. Look for opportunities around you, in your field of expertise and interest. If you keep an open eye and an open mind, you never know what possibilities you might find.

GirlPreneurs see and seize opportunities.

Love What You Do

Now that we have reached the point in this story where I found myself in the position of starting my own business, we thought it might be a good time to ask you to think about where you are in your own journey. Do you have an idea for a business that you think is unique and marketable? Are you ready to take on the challenges of starting a business? It's always a smart idea to ask yourself questions to gauge if you think you might be ready to start your own adventure as a GirlPreneur.

When I started, I had a lot to learn. I knew that I had a good idea and from the research that I had gathered, it looked like my idea had good market viability and there was basically no competition. But beyond that, I was starting from scratch. I had a graduate degree in social work, but I had no experience with the concepts or processes of starting a business. Like most entrepreneurs, I had to learn everything as I went along.

This book is packed with information and tips that I learned in a very short amount of

Confessions of a GirlPRENEUR | 65

time that helped me become a successful female founder.

The first thing I would say is—you gotta love what you do! This is the single most important principle in business. Success as an entrepreneur ultimately comes down to how badly you want it. These are practical skills and habits that are the fundamental ingredients for success in any area of life, be it academic, social, business, the arts or sports. By applying these attitudes and habits, your chances of solving problems, establishing a good reputation, growing a company, creating a masterpiece or staying fit are greatly increased because you understand that everything starts and stops with you. Anything after that can be taught, acquired, mentored, bought or borrowed. But passion and love—that's your job, GirlPreneur, and it must come from your heart and soul.

Businesses are supposed to make money. That's your perk for the blood, sweat and tears that you give to your business. You can develop what you believe to be the best business in the world, but if you don't love what you do, you will have a very difficult time putting in the hours and sacrifices to stick with it on a day-to-day basis.

Now is the time to start asking yourself some critical questions: Why do you want to go into business? Is this something that just occurred to you while sitting at your desk, bored out of your wits at your job, or have you been dreaming of this moment for years, socking away money in the hopes of owning your own company?

There are plenty of advantages to being a GirlPreneur, but only you can know if it's the right decision for you. This is the stage where you get to think long and hard about how your decision to become an entrepreneur will impact your lifestyle, your family, your finances, your potential love life, your *life*. So you had best be prepared.

Think-Aloud GirlPreneur Pros:

- ✓ You are your own boss and call the shots. Enough said.
- ✓ You own the show and get to build a zippy business.
- ✓ You make your own schedule.
- ✓ You have more opportunity for financial gain.
- ✓ You will meet amazing people, many of them on the same journey as you.
- ✓ You create the work environment.
- ✓ You can bring your dog to work.
- ✓ You can set the dress code and tone for your work environment.
- ✓ You may have tax advantages.

Think-Aloud GirlPreneur Cons:

✓ You will work a lot.
✓ Your social life might suffer.
✓ Your love life might suffer.
✓ You have no guarantees of business success.
✓ You will experience stress daily.
✓ You may have to borrow money to start up.
✓ You will have to keep abreast of the competition.
✓ Your mom will worry about you a lot.
✓ You'll have many moments when you question your sanity.

If after weighing the pros and cons of entrepreneurship you have decided that starting a business is right for you, then get ready! You are going to work harder than you ever have, or could imagine you would, but if you do it right, it will be the most amazing journey.

If you are making this decision to go into business, you probably know if you have the temperament or personality for it. What does that mean? Why do passion and determination matter to your business venture? Because your attitudes and habits might well be the determining factors in whether or not you succeed in opening and staying in business. Successful entrepreneurs often have an unusual amount of determination, persistence, passion, focus and drive.

Your positive attitudes and habits will give you a leg up when it comes to toughing it out. That's important because the first years can be rough. The percentage of small businesses that fail in the first few years is high. Those statistics can be discouraging. But it is important to know up front that you'll need all your grit and drive to kick through those early start-up years.

When I started my business, one of the first habits I learned that worked for me was rising early. I needed that time in the early hours to organize and prepare. When most people were just arriving at their offices, I was ready to go and laser-focused. I efficiently and purposefully mapped out my work day. Getting up early ultimately increased my confidence because I felt prepared for the day ahead.

We all have different strengths, different skills and different interests that will determine what type of company we build and how and when we go about it. No two companies are alike unless you are opening a franchise, but even then, there is more variety than you might think. There is no single template for building a business, but the tools to help you succeed are very similar regardless of the type of business you are founding.

Business is not necessarily complicated, but it does require habits and approaches that anyone can employ. Applied with diligence, these habits and approaches can greatly increase your chances of success. If you approach your business idea, goal setting, business plan practices, sales and marketing campaigns and financial measurement systems with these habits in place, then you're bound to find solutions that work for your particular business. And by the way, these habits can be applied to almost any endeavor to improve your likelihood of success.

Persistence, Determination, Courage, Focus, Confidence, Resilience and Passion:

Acquiring these characteristics is a matter of fostering them. It is the try-try again rule; the more you practise the better you get. **Persistence**, the more often you are persistent, the more persistent you can become. The more chances you have to exercise your **Determination**, the stronger your sense of it will be the next time. The potential for **Courageous** action opens you up to facing and then conquering your fears; then you have found courage! **Focusing** requires discipline and practising careful attentiveness. **Confidence** is gained through practising, over and over, believing in yourself and in your decisions. **Resilience** means you don't give up when the going gets tough. **Passion** you are both born with and can fuel the fire of.

That is a lot to think about, but don't let that deter you. The key is to make a smart, calculated and informed decision (which you will!) to ensure that you have what it takes to weather the storm. GirlPreneurs always do our due diligence before we jump in. And then when we jump, we jump in with both feet.

And let's not forget the thrill of it all! Entrepreneurship has been described as an extreme sport. Anyone who contemplates going into business for themselves likely has a bit of the thrill-seeker in them. Maybe it was skateboarding down Cherry Street, the steepest street in your neighborhood that turned you into a dare-devil. Maybe it was taking Jane Laney's double dare to eat an ant in the elementary school playground. If you had the intense focus required to skate down Cherry Street with the passion of the boarder, if you had the determination to one-up Jane Laney and the cleverness to pretend to eat the ant, afterwards enjoying your new ant-eating cachet, you are endowed with the skills for business. Focus, determination, passion and, persistence, with a bit of showmanship thrown in, means you are on your way to success.

To me, business, is a lot like downhill skiing. As a little girl at the top of a ski hill in the Gatineau Hills outside Ottawa, I knew that one way or another I had to get myself back down on these two long, flat boards. At first, it felt impossible. But I taught myself that with baby glides, I could work my way down the hill. I learned to persevere through my fears and got used to taking things one step (or ski) at a time. I fell a lot in the beginning, but I was determined to make it down. So I just did it again and again. I eventually became good enough to sail down the hill and then get back into the lift line because I wanted more.

And it doesn't end. I like to try to continue to challenge myself and help out in my community. I joined the Canadian Ski Patrol in 2014 because I've been a long-time skier on those hills and I know the lay of the land and I felt I probably could be of help. It's my thing. I love that level of confidence you need and the competence that I feel as I soar down a steep slope. By August I am already craving ski season and I'll ski right up until April! Moguls and the black diamond hills have become my metaphors for the obstacles and challenges that I have to pivot around and negotiate in the real world. And sometimes, even with years of practice and experience I still fall, and I still need to pick myself up, point the boards down the hill and keep on going.

Most things in life are possible if you want them bad enough. Passion is the spark that gets things going, and it can also be the fuel that keeps you moving forward when times get tough. You might have to go forward, go sideways—even go backwards sometimes.

As entrepreneurs we love what we do but what differentiates us from others is that we try to turn our mistakes into lessons learned in order to avoid making the same mistakes over and over. We get back on the horse, or the ski hill, or tackle the business problem in front of us to come up with a winning solution. We do not easily give up and failure is not an option.

Becoming Financially Savvy

Ok girls, now it's time to talk about your money. And that is no easy task for some of us. I don't know about you, but before I started a business, I was dreadful with money. I had no concept of its value, or it might be more honest to say, I had no respect for its value. I was a chequebook balancing nightmare. At the time, if I'd said to my mother that I was going out to save the penguins, she would have believed it more readily than she would have believed that I could start a business and be successful at it. My family are still surprised, not only that I became a successful entrepreneur, but that I did it while handling my own money.

It wasn't that I was a big spender. I wasn't. I just didn't see any use for money in and of itself. Money had always been a way to get to do stuff, like going out at night with your friends to the pubs and clubs. And my friends were the same. We were all quite communal with our cash. I'd borrow, they'd borrow; whoever had just been paid and was flush would pick up the tab. We were young and care-free and just wanted to have fun. If we didn't have

73

any money, we'd just pick up more shifts and get some more.

This is a charming way to live, but it's not going to work if you are going into business. Business requires that you become financially prudent. A business requires financial astuteness or you will big bad fail. Don't worry, if I could learn financial prudence, so can you! I was able, over time, to teach myself not only how to be good with money, but how to make it, save it and then make the saved part generate more.

I started my private practice because I needed to work to support myself. At the forefront of my mind from the day I started was the financial goal of supporting myself. It really was that simple.

What launched my business was financial vigilance. Knowing my costs, I was able to calculate the revenue that I needed to bring in each month. I knew the minimum amount of revenue that I needed from my practice in order to avoid having to (gulp) pack it in and go to work for somebody else. Knowing those numbers kept me motivated to perform and stay ahead of financial doom. So I put my head down and resolved that I was going to make that x amount of dollars to cover my costs. I could do it!

Then I had to calculate what my budget meant in terms of cash flow. I needed to know how many sessions I had to do in order to make my rent. I needed to map it out in actual revenue. For example, if I needed to make $3,000 to cover my basic costs, I knew that I had to bring in at least $3,000 in revenue—but how could I break this down into bite-sized pieces?

I did the math. And it was very simple math. Each of my clients paid $60 a session, therefore $3,000 divided by $60 meant that I had to do 50 sessions per month. Although this was far from a full work load, the combination of marketing my services and then providing the services ended up keeping me very busy! Having an exact understanding of my costs versus my revenue not only kept me from pending financial disaster, it gave me a concrete and easy-to-understand goal to work towards. I had to do 50 counselling sessions per month at $60.00 per hour in order to stay afloat.

Although I set lofty goals (really dreams) of making $100K a year, at the very beginning I kept it super simple: within a year, I wanted to be able to support myself full time as an entrepreneur. I learned to enjoy delayed gratification. I also learned to keep things simple because I was building something bigger and better that required acute and daily attention to detail.

In the beginning, I didn't use any fancy accounting or bookkeeping packages. I had to teach myself basic finance while simultaneously building my business. How much were my costs? How much did I need to bring in? How did this translate directly into clients and contracts? The process wasn't radical mathematics. I just used very simple arithmetic. I charted how much I needed to make to meet my costs, broken down into bite-size metrics of how I was going to make this money. I kept careful track of my expenses. And I saved every receipt and categorized it pronto. I kept files on my desk with each expense category, put the receipts into folders and tracked them every month.

When you first start out in business, avoid outsourcing anything unless absolutely necessary. This isn't just an exercise in frugality, it is vital that you learn every intimate detail about how your business works. Learning how to do everything yourself will make you a savvy, knowledgeable entrepreneur. And this is especially important if you choose to grow your business and hire staff. You will want to have a base understanding of the many different areas of your business in order to hire and effectively manage staff.

And the great news is that you can get a lot of advice for free just by being friendly, curious and asking questions. For example, by taking a business contact out for coffee, you can often get all kinds of free advice for just the cost of a double mocha latte.

New entrepreneurs sometimes think they need fancy stuff. But you don't. If you really need someone to help set up your accounts, you might hire an accountant fresh out of graduate school. Usually, you don't need anything complicated, other than to be knowledgeable about all of the various aspects of your business. Start simple. Practice cost management.

You can build a million-dollar company and have no money because your costs are so high. On the other hand, the GirlPreneur with the $500K company might be rolling in dough because she knows how to control her costs and make a great profit.

Many of us have scrimped, struggled, and marketed our way to success. If we can do it, so can you. Our early stories will likely mirror where you are at now. GirlPreneurs, look for the stories of female founders who have become successful and seek out mentorship from established female entrepreneurs!

As the saying goes, it takes a village to create a successful entrepreneur! None of us become successful alone.

Bootstrapping Your Business

You now know how I created the service I wanted to deliver. Now we need to look at how I turned the service into a functioning business. We need to talk about financing. I was clipping along for months in a classic one-person counseling practice model, and then along came Peter and I had my "aha! moment" when I realized I could turn my passion into something bigger and create the business of my dreams. I was going to take my private practice and build it into an industry-leading company.

But how did I finance this business? I used the bootstrapping business model to build the Trauma Management Group. It is a model I wholeheartedly support for the early stages of building your business until you are able to prove that you can attract and retain paying customers.

Bootstrapping is built on cash flow financing: you start to build your business with money you already have or that you bring in from revenue. For example, when I began my trauma counseling business, I built it based on the revenue that we were bringing in. Every time we had surplus cash (profit), we hired a new contract person, waited until we were again in a profit-generating position and then hired the next contract person and so on. Initially, I used the bank for overdraft protection in the event that I had cash flow issues. I never had money from investors, so I didn't have to give away any equity (ownership) in my company. From the day I started the business to the day I sold it, I was 100 percent owner; it was *mine*.

It's not that I'm opposed to early-stage financing; however, it is not easy to secure funding, and it involves a lot of time-consuming and expensive legal elements that can distract your focus from building your business. And the minute you take investment capital you lose equity in your company. Think about this before rushing to seek investors, because an investor becomes a partner/owner in *your* business. And their primary goal is to ensure they get their money back—and then some!—not necessarily in building your dream business.

Every successful business operates on a similar metric: Sell more than you spend to bring in a profit. There are some businesses, such as manufacturing or retail, that start out in a deficit due to high initial overhead costs. Unless you absolutely must have the capital in the early stages of business development (for example, if you need equipment or inventory to build your start-up), start with your own revenue-generating cycle based on the slow and systematic hustle of sales and cash flow.

Some entrepreneurs think that if they can secure outside capital (angel or venture capital financing), it increases the worth of their business because someone has given them an outside valuation of their company's worth. Recently, I was at an event where the owners of a start-up were bragging about how they had secured $500K in investment capital. Yet they admitted that they had not secured any customers or sales. I remember saying, "Great, now you have proven that you can raise money; but imagine where your business would be if you had put that energy—they had spent hundreds of hours hustling investors—into hustling customers!" Plus, the investor took 25 percent of their company. As we all know, there are always strings attached when you take money from others.

By definition, creating a business involves risk. But caution in business is actually a very good thing with a well-organized business plan. Being methodical and building a company with a solid base of revenue-to-cost-to-profit is smart. It is wise to be reluctant to take money from investors until you can prove to yourself and to others that you have a product or a service that has solid sales.

And besides it isn't easy to get investors, especially for GirlPreneurs. In the current landscape, the majority of angel and venture capital investors are male, and they often don't recognize the value and opportunity in female-generated businesses. And as women we often start, run and grow our businesses differently than our male counterparts. These two factors make it more difficult for women to access capital, again making bootstrapping not only a good option, but often the only option.

Running up your overhead is not a good idea for an emerging entrepreneur. Keep your costs extremely low, work to secure paying customers and start building on this cash flow cycle. I ran the counseling company out of a spare room in my apartment for nearly a year before finally taking on the expense of renting an office. Even when I did, I shared the office with a business colleague to reduce costs.

I kept my expenses—personal and professional—as low as possible in its start-up phase. In the beginning years, my assistants made more than I did. I drove an old beater of a car. I shopped at consignment stores. I shared office space. And every penny of profit I made I reinvested in the company so I could hire more staff who could perform more work and help me put the company into the lead position that it eventually achieved. This is the bootstrap model. And it works.

Aside from bootstrap financing, there are other ways to raise early capital for your company. Your local government may have a chamber of commerce or board of trade that can provide listings of the various private and public sector groups that offer start-up funding. You can also turn to your local entrepreneur / business ecosystem for networks of funders. Also, the internet has many crowd source (crowd funding) sites to pitch your idea. As always, follow due diligence in your research to safeguard you and your business.

Building a business is not an exact science. The key concept is being open, flexible and adaptive to using the right mix of the various funding sources for your company, of which bootstrapping is always going to be a useful option.

Bootstrapping is a business model and it is also a philosophy. Bootstrapping promotes the concept of being financially prudent and savvy. It's not about how much revenue you make, but rather the fine balance between revenue and expenses, with the goal of generating profit.

Your First Year in Business

Your first year in business is about survival. The success of your business will depend on that most basic business equation: You need to bring in more revenue than you have in costs. Any surplus is your profit for a job well done. The goal is to make more revenue while also keeping your costs low. The greater your profit, the more money you should put aside to cover cash flow. This profit will allow you to keep your business operational if you have a few lean months and it will also be useful if you decide to grow your company as growth requires cash.

Financial facts that matter:

- ✓ Know your costs in detail.
- ✓ Know how much revenue you need to bring in to cover costs.
- ✓ What is your break-even point for profitability?
- ✓ Control your costs to the bare minimum.
- ✓ Hustle like crazy to promote sales.

For a business to go from survive to thrive in the first year, it often comes down to how you manage your cash flow. Most businesses are built in a fairly similar fashion, yet can operate on many levels. The core principle is that a business must have a product or service that others place value on and want to buy. You don't need to own a company that generates $10 million annually to be a GirlPreneur. You might make family meals and sell them after school. You might work from home making beaded jewelry and sell it online. You might have developed a software prototype for a Fortune 500 company. You may have 2, 10, or 100 employees—or no employees. You may be local, national or international. You may have shareholders or you may be a one-woman show. You don't have to be big to be a viable business.

For the most part, the setting up, structuring and operating of a business requires similar procedures and practices. There are volumes of business books and blogs specific to each stage of the business cycle that may be an additional resource for you. So I suggest that you: Read. Read. Read. Put your pride aside when starting out. Find the right people and ask a lot of questions. And the questions you ask yourself about your business are the most important questions of all.

The GirlPreneur Pre-Launch Checklist:

- ✓ Is this business right for me?
- ✓ Can I see getting out of bed every morning for the next 5 years to do this?
- ✓ Do I have the expertise to make the business work?
- ✓ Have I investigated my competition?
- ✓ Do I have the necessary capital to start? Have I considered loans/grants?
- ✓ Am I familiar with price setting strategies?
- ✓ Will I work from home, or rent or share space?
- ✓ Am I starting the business alone or do I have a partner?
- ✓ Should I incorporate?

And any other questions that come to mind that are specific to your start up business.

GirlPreneurs sometimes think that building a business is a complex undertaking. But I assure you, it is not. If you make the wrong decision and you land on your butt? So what! Most successful GirlPreneurs have bounced off our butts dozens of times to get to where we are. Failures and missteps are the potholes on the road traveled by the GirlPreneur. We don't let them derail, defeat or define us. We pick up our heels, dust off our pantsuits and carry on.

I was a social worker with zero business acumen, yet I built an industry-leading company. I followed my passion for helping others while making a living for myself. I realized that I did not have all the answers and that I would have to learn as I went along. I made lots of mistakes because I took lots of chances.

I was my own bank, for the most part. I was the payroll clerk, the marketer, the collection agency and accounts receivable, all in one. I learned very clearly how my business worked. I also learned where I could borrow money to cover off cash flow.

Even for a profitable startup company, it is not unusual to have cash flow issues. On your books you may be owed $100K in receivables, but your bank account is in the negative to the tune of $100K. When it comes time to pay the staff and the bills, you must have cash in the bank or a very good line of credit and overdraft.

I developed a great relationship with my bank manager, who got to know me on a first-name basis. I would take our income statement, our receivables and our balance sheet to the bank. Usually within minutes I'd be in the bank manager's office saying I needed a $20K+ increase in my credit line. I would display the reports that showed we had just made $100K in sales and had $75K coming in this week from clients. But I needed to pay my staff this Friday.

I had to do this a half dozen times over the course of my business ownership. My staff never knew the pressure I was under, and they didn't need to. But I have many vivid memories of nail biting, teeth clenching, insomnia and sheer panic as I tried to meet payroll some weeks! I was totally leveraged.

I remember one summer evening, I was tossing and turning and couldn't get to sleep. It was a Monday night and I had to meet payroll that Friday and we were $60K short. At 1 a.m., in my nightie and flip-flops, I went outside and paced up and down my street thinking that I was totally screwed. I'd never missed payroll, not once. After pacing for a half hour, I came to the realization that I was going to have to call every client that owed us money. I would personally go to all their offices to collect what they owed. We met payroll that week by the skin of our teeth.

One of the main reasons businesses fail is because of poor cash flow; not having the money to meet the bills that start to pile up. Credit will only get you so far. Eventually if you don't have the money to pay your bills, your company is going to start to fail. I realized that if I was going to grow (also known as scale) my company financially I would have to have surplus cash to work with.

My private practice was my tutorial year. I learned through experience to understand the financials on a daily basis. I had mastered expenses, but now I was so busy I couldn't do it all myself.

So when the big revenue cheques started coming in, I kept living on my budget, and used the surplus to hire staff. All my marketing was paying off. The Trauma Management Group now started to strategically and slowly staff up. It was daunting to have big overhead costs and people depending on me! As a CEO, you know how fragile your business is and how responsible you need to be when others depend on you. The responsibility can at times be overwhelming.

My first administrator, Cindy, was a young, fresh, unskilled gal. All she really knew how to do was answer the phone and do word processing. But she was affordable because she was inexperienced. She was smart, honest and hard-working. I sent her on a bookkeeping course because I needed her to watch our finances the way I had been doing, but on a larger scale. She was to keep track of all issues related to money. During those early years, I made less than my secretaries. Why? Because I knew that I had to reinvest every dollar that I made back into the company to hire more great staff to help me grow the business. And so the cycle continued.

Within months, the company began to experience significant growth. And with this came significant revenue increases and also significant overhead costs. I needed to see a snapshot of the financial operations daily to be sure that we were managing our growth.

Cindy was able to produce reports that told me how much revenue we were bringing in, from where, and how much it cost us to service each file. And I could see this information updated every single day. Remember, you can't run a company if you don't have money. As the founder, it is your job to stay on top of things.

If you are a bootstrap entrepreneur, scale the company up when and if you have the cash. Except for administrative staff, I hired only people that I could bill out. Ninety percent of my staff were billable staff so that I could build their costs into my contracts. And don't count your chickens before they hatch. You may think you are going to get a contract, and then something changes. Your client goes belly up or you don't get the work. Avoid hiring or outlaying money before you actually have a signed contract. I had to learn this the hard way.

We customized the reports Cindy produced so they gave me the information I needed. She would provide an income statement by category of monies owing to the company, a receivables report showing accounts owing in 0-30 day, 30-50 day, and 90 day increments, a balance sheet providing information on the overall assets and liabilities of the company, and a general ledger, which tracked in detail all the expenses of the company. These financial reports were then compared to our marketing reports so that we could determine how we were doing and in each category of the company.

So for example, if we were growing in our corporate contracts area, I would be able to provide good feedback to the staff person who marketed our services to this sector. And to the contrary, if our costs were too high, I would be able to pin point where, and then be able to provide feedback to the staff person responsible for contract management.

And I would sometimes ask to see the bills for the month. I would scrutinize everything, because that's what good entrepreneurs do. Why did we pay $2K a month for gas? Why did we have receivables coming in on sixty to ninety days? Your goal is to have thirty day receivables. Sure, sometimes holidays interfere. But that should have been an exception. Lags in payment, which affects cash flow, can kill small companies. That is why you have to have accessible cash savings and credit lines, and why it is important to have good client relationships so that you can call and inquire about overdue accounts.

The company began doing really well a couple of years after we started, and our revenue streams became more defined and secure. I bought a house for $220K. I did a small renovation and it was now valued at $500K. Then I bought our office building. The bank leveraged my house to buy the building. And so the leverage cycle continued. In the end, the bank manager always loaned me the money. She knew I was good for it. And she could have seized my house and other assets if I wasn't.

All GirlPreneurs know that risk is an inherent part of building a business, that when you venture out on your own, you're risking it all to follow your passion in pursuit of success. There is no guarantee that you will be successful, but the challenge is worth it.

Once you start to delve into money management, you will learn more about income statements, balance statements, general ledger reports and receivables reports. The financial reports are generated from your accounting system and provide you with the details you need to understand the past, present and future financial operation of your company.

I could go on and on about financial reports but I won't. It is not that type of book. What I want to impart to you are the concepts of becoming financially astute in business. When you understand these concepts, you will know and understand the financial status of your company each and every day and know intimately how your cash flow cycle works.

Your financial reports will become regular bedtime reading. You will be climbing under your lovely duvet covers with a glass of wine or tea and your stack of reports. Believe it or not, you will enjoy reading them because they are all about you and your beautiful business.

Shout Out

As a GirlPreneur, you are either a natural networker or you will become one in a hurry. Any time you walk out that door, you are an ambassador for your brand. You are driven to share your product/service because you love what you have created. And you love sharing. It's more fun than keeping something to yourself.

Keep this in mind on your journey to GirlPreneurship. Once you go into business, your contact circle is going to grow exponentially. You'll be attending business meetings and charity galas, interviewing people and going to conferences and trade shows. Ask for contact information for everyone you meet. Keep this information organized, and personalize it so that you remember who each person is as well as their special information. You'll want to be able to easily contact that friend of your cousin who happens to know a great source for materials for your business. You never know when you will need information about someone or something.

Networking is very much about goodwill. The word-of-mouth network is invaluable. It's what sells products and services. As a successful entrepreneur, you don't go in for one-off deals; you want to build relationships that create customers for life. A happy customer will promote and sell your products for you. Networks and businesses grow on goodwill.

People within your network have the potential to open doors for you and become your allies and ambassadors. They will help promote your business by saying nice things and be part of your entrepreneurial support system. Your networks can help you get your message out, link you to new customers and give your business more exposure. A network will also give you people to call on those days when you feel isolated and in need of guidance.

Just the other day, a leading industry colleague referred me for a speaking engagement at a business conference. When the organizers called him and he wasn't available, he gave them my name. That's the power of networking.

Any social situation is an opportunity to network. Every time you step out your front door, it's a chance to talk about what you do and engage someone new to find out if you can help each other in some way. Networking is different from a regular relationship because it's strategic and purposeful, but it still must always be genuine.

For example, with the Trauma Management Group, I built powerful networks with heads of corporations, emergency medical services staff and people in various government ministries because we would benefit from being able to call upon one another.

When you attend a networking event, keep initial conversations open to encourage dialogue. Give the person you are talking to the chance to ask questions. I would say something like, "Hi, I'm Fiona Gilligan with the Trauma Management Group." I deliberately left out my position so that the person I was meeting would be curious to ask me questions and a conversation could start.

The key to networking is building engagement and exchanging goodwill. By talking this way you'll find out if you can help one another's business. As the conversation goes back and forth, be sure to provide clear, concise information about your company but never breach confidentiality. I would often refer to current events in general terms. ("Do you remember the train derailment that happened last month? Our company was hired to provide the trauma counselling.") Often, the other person would find a personal context and respond with a comment like, "Oh really? My brother was one of the emergency workers on site." You'll be amazed at how small the world is when you start to network. There are often very few degrees of separation between people.

Once you've started to chat, you may want to ask for an introduction. "Please feel free to let your brother know about our company—or would you like us to do an outreach call to tell him about our services?" Keep in mind that, at a social event, if you are networking most other people are too. Don't worry about talking up your business and suggesting a follow up conversation. Most people are doing the same. The key is to avoid one-way conversations or giving the impression that you are there strictly for business purposes. By encouraging friendly chit-chat around the exchange of information about your business there could be many lead-ins to follow-up opportunities.

If you love what you do and your passion is obvious, networking can be fun and effortless. For most of us, it is a learned skill. The more you get out and talk about your business, the more confident you become. Networking is an essential part of selling because people tend to buy from those they know and trust.

Networking tips:

- ✓ Be yourself.
- ✓ Be friendly, engaging and sincere.
- ✓ Be confident.
- ✓ Introduce yourself and begin a dialogue.
- ✓ Be concise. Have your business pitch down to less than 30 seconds.
- ✓ Ask questions. Be interested and interesting.
- ✓ Hand out your business card or direct people to your website.
- ✓ Ask for their contact information and introductions to new networks.
- ✓ Follow up within a few days after meeting someone of interest.

When networking, there are three types of people you will want to seek out who can help and support you in your journey.

The Mentor: Ideally, this will be an entrepreneur who is established with proven success. A mentor can become a close ally who will share her secrets and tips and teach you all she learned from her successes and failures.

The Peer: This is someone at roughly the same business stage as you, or slightly ahead, who is living through similar experiences. Your commonality of experience will bind you and if you are at similar building stages, you can share resources.

The Sponsor: This is usually an established entrepreneur who is well respected and actively involved in the business ecosystems. A sponsor can help you open networks that you could not easily open on your own. She can also help spread the word about your business within her networks. The right sponsor can speed up your company's progress by months, if not years.

Networking faux pas can happen to the best of us. Networking events can offer perfect opportunities for embarrassment. It is easy to make an awkward and embarrassing gaffe. Below are some typical characters whose behaviours you may want to avoid.

The mobile-device addict: People who are more engaged with their smart phone than the person in front of them are rude. Put your devices away and focus on the people in front of you. If you must tweet or check messages, do it discreetly or excuse yourself.

The chronic salesperson: No networking event is complete without the person who is there to sell and just can't stop pitching. This person doesn't know how to switch it off, and as a result she turns off everyone around her.

The distracted networker: This person can't maintain eye contact because she is always on the lookout for someone more important so that she can trade up. She is an overt opportunist who will quickly be revealed to everyone as shallow and insincere.

The monopolizer: In Victorian times, the person who never stopped talking was called a bore. Networking conversations should be short and light. Don't take too much of someone's time; everyone has other people to meet. Keep strong opinions to yourself and avoid hot topics that could alienate people.

The flirt: One of the best ways to lose your credibility is to sex up your talk or behavior at a networking function. You want to be taken seriously, so don't play the sexy girly-girl card. Dress appropriately and speak professionally. Exude confidence and smarts.

The drunk: Networking events usually include alcohol and it is very easy to get caught up in the moment and drink too much. There is no better way to kill your reputation than getting drunk and losing your inhibitions. Your credibility could be ruined immediately, for the present and into the future. You will be remembered for all the wrong reasons. Networking events are not meant to be nights out on the town. You are there on business.

And Now...
Putting it all Together

So that's the condensed version of my personal story, about my parents, my childhood, funny things that happened along the way, and ultimately, how I got started in business, and what I learned and the odds I had to overcome. I thought this was important to include because becoming a GirlPreneur is as much about the journey as it is the destination. The journey for all entrepreneurs is full of mountains and valleys, twists and turns and the power of sharing our stories is how we learn from one another. My journey to GirlPreneurship was circuitous and surprising, and I learned much along the way.

Storytelling is powerful. In the following chapters, we have created mock scenarios for each of the main business concepts so that you can gain a greater understanding of how to put it all together. By this stage you are hopefully inspired and motivated to continue to move forward to becoming a GirlPreneur. These case studies explain the different business phases through fictional characters and their startups.

In Chapter 17, Molly has a burning idea to take her passion and love of frozen juice pops and see if she can turn it into a business. It is a great idea, but what are the steps she needs to take to determine if her business is market worthy?

In Chapter 18, Carly O. and Avery explore the importance of goal setting as they build their film production company. They share with us how they moved forward towards business success by setting small and big goals.

In Chapter 19, Alice and Janey show us how important having a business plan is to getting launched into a successful venture.

And, in Chapter 20, Serena shows us how to successfully market and sell her micro beer company. She then goes on, in Chapter 21, to share with us her trade secrets.

What will *your* story be?

The Idea Phase

Name: Molly
Business: Molly's Pops
Location: Atlanta, GA
Age: 27

It's midnight and you're still up at your computer reading about frozen juices on wooden sticks. Why? You're not in 7th grade. No, but a year ago when you were in Austin, Texas you came across an artisanal ice pop truck. It was the coolest thing (no pun intended) you'd ever seen. You and your friends ate a dozen of them and tried all the flavours—Lemongrass-Ginger, Chocolate-Strawberry and the Mint-Almond-Coconut—while sitting under the willow trees on the downtown street. And you weren't the only ones; there were huge lines, but they zipped right along. The frozen pops were divine, and the best thing of all was that they were made with all-natural ingredients and the truck was a smashing color of pink.

Now, Austin is a pretty balmy climate, but you also live in a pretty warm spot, Atlanta, Georgia, or

101

Hotlanta, as it's known locally. And people here like artisanal. There is even a pickle store where you can buy hand-crafted pickles by the spear.

So you've been daydreaming about making frozen Green Tea Chai-pops and Matcha-pops and selling them from a truck on hot June days, but you've also been researching the market in Atlanta to find out if there are any ice pop vendors and you haven't come across any. Why not? You're not sure why not. There was a girl making paletas (the Mexican equivalent of ice pops) from a truck, but she moved to Athens with her boyfriend. You heard they were opening up shop there. Ice pops are a hot trend. The biz mags have been touting the low start-up costs of small-batch artisanal products. There are gelato stores here, but no handmade frozen juice pops as yet. It seems you could be the first to splash onto the market, as it were. That's called a beachhead—when you are the first one to corner the marketplace before your competitors. It's hard to compete with a beachhead business, unless they are terrible business managers or their product or service stinks.

You already have a product. And it's stellar! All the customers say so. For the past six months you've been making small batches of pops in your kitchen, packaging them and selling them on the weekends at two farmers markets, sharing space in a stall with another vendor. After a few months of selling to friends, you didn't want to take chances,

Confessions of a GirlPRENEUR | 103

so you got your food business license for market vendors as well as your seller's permit.

The packaging design is cool. You found eco sleeves that you bought in bulk. You slide the pops into the sleeves, lay them down in boxes in sets of 20, and put them into carry coolers. Believe it or not, even packaging your product is great fun!

At last, that large deep freezer you inherited from your aunt that has been sitting empty in your basement is being used. The farmer's markets have been good exposure. "Molly's Pops" have been selling out a good number of weekends. Especially on sunny weekends, of course! Because the pops are made without preservatives, they taste best when they are fresh. You don't keep them from one week to the next. When there are leftovers, dependable roommates are happy to polish them off. The Chocolate-Banana-Rama is especially popular with kids; all the flavours are popular with your roommates. Free is the catch there.

But fresh produce sure isn't free. It's pretty pricey, so it helps that your brother happens to be a small distributor for local farms. He's the one who encouraged you to try your recipes at the market in the first place. Through him, you've been able to source good fruit and dairy at reasonable prices, although pickups and deliveries have been tricky to arrange. At least you have a good relationship with your main supplier! And the terms are agreeable to both of you. You haven't quit your copywriting job yet, but with the money from the weekend sales you've hired a friend to design a catchy, colourful logo. You've already ordered business cards, postcards and a party price-list pamphlet. The last item was a whim, but all those Chocolate-Banana-Rama–eating tots have parents who seemed desperate for fun new birthday party food and latched onto the idea of having a Molly's Pops stand at their next party. When you mentioned this to a friend, she shouted, "That's it! A pop-up Molly's Pops Stand!" She thought it was very clever of her to come up with that idea—it was!

So you put together your own pop stand and hired a friend to work it. The awning is a brilliant colour of watermelon pink. The mini freezer-truck is the cutest thing ever, white with "Molly's Pops" written on the side in the same pink. One Saturday, a woman rushing by the stall with a load of flowers in her arms waved her card and yelled, "Please call me." Her card indicated she was an event planner. As she rushed off she yelled out—"Office parties… conferences…pop stands." You haven't had time to call her yet, but she gave you food for thought. (You want to have your pops in a row, so to speak, before you talk to her. You want to make sure you have answers to any questions she might have.)

Now you're thinking that perhaps the event route is a great avenue to pursue. You're not sure you're ready or that it's necessary to pay rent for

Confessions of a GirlPRENEUR | 105

a retail space. This will require more research because it is a larger enterprise. You have a lot to investigate. How would you produce enough juice pops to please an entire ballroom of 500? Your pops sell for $3 each. Your freezer holds about 2,000 of them. The issue is always the melt time. Cream based pops melt faster, so they have to be the first ones in and out. According to the chamber of commerce, Atlanta hosts hundreds of conferences and trade shows a year.

Now you're holding down two jobs, which is making life crazy, but for some reason you don't mind. In fact, even though you are often exhausted, you are really invigorated by all the details about your business. You've always been a detail-oriented person—that's the nature of copywriting—but this is different.

This is exciting and you seem to spend most of your free time making lists and talking to people about the Molly Pops potential. You feel like you might need to take some time to study this opportunity and talk to someone who has started up a business from scratch. Someone who can give you advice, who can look at what you've started to write down on paper objectively and see if it makes good business sense. Can a pop-up Pops stand be profitable? Is serving the event industry a good target market? Your Pops are popular, but how do you know if it's a viable idea to try and open up a full-blown business? What you need is some good old-fashioned advice from one of your business networking mentors. That's it. You're going to call her and set up a meeting.

So you meet with your mentor. She gives you lots of excellent advice.

Your mentor loves research. She believes in making decision trees and listing the pros and cons of starting the business. She suggests taking the idea and putting it through the evaluation process. She explains that by taking time at the beginning of the journey on the road to GirlPreneurship, by carefully and systematically exploring every angle of building the business, you are going to increase the your odds of success.

She goes on to suggest gathering as much information as possible on the idea and its merits. Ask questions. What is the target market? Who are your competitors? What are the start-up costs? Where will the initial capital come from? What physical set-up is needed? What's the monthly overhead? What are the short-term gains and long-range benefits? Are there any government regulations you need to be aware of? What is the cost-to-profit ratio? What's the growth potential? Does a lawyer need to assist with any legal aspects of getting started?

Those are a lot of questions that need answers! So although you may be in a hurry to get your pops

Confessions of a GirlPRENEUR | 107

to a bigger market, you need to first be exhaustive with your research.

Your mentor goes on to suggest that at this point you need time and distance to gain perspective. This is an important step. You need to allow the variables to percolate to see things clearly so that you can make a successful decision. Go visit your aunt. Go to the spa. Go do something fun for a few days where you are not actively working on your business idea. Because once you jump in it will be with both feet and there will be no looking back.

When you feel you have researched to the hilt and you've visited Aunt Maisy twice, it's time to make your decision tree and apply all that research and creative stewing to methodically write out what you learned.

Start by defining the problem, then make two columns, "pros" and "cons." These columns state in broad terms the advantages and disadvantages of moving forward with your business decision. Take a week putting together your decision tree, going back to it daily to refine it as your thoughts evolve. During this step you will be adding, deleting and modifying your pros and cons so that you can arrive at a confident and well-thought-out decision.

The decision tree will give you a very good sense of whether you are ready to move forward with your decision or whether you should wait until further research convinces you one way or the other for certain.

Your mentor explains that the most important next step for any entrepreneur is to be able to pitch their idea. You need to define the idea for the business in two or three sentences. The pitch should contain all the essential, pertinent information about the venture. What makes your product unique? What problem will it solve? Who will buy it? You need to fine tune the pitch until it rolls off the tip of your tongue, because only when you know your business and what you are selling can you truly sell it to others. She says to test the pitch out on people to see if they understand it and to fine tune it if they don't.

So you give yours a try. "Molly's Pops is a company specializing in home-made gourmet frozen juice pops made to order for event and party planning businesses. Whether it's a kids' party, a wedding or a conference, we create the ice pops especially for your theme. We even provide beautiful, high quality pop-up pop stands as part of the package."

Short and sweet (Ha). *Not bad,* your mentor says. *Short and sweet (ha ha). Maybe you could add "serving the greater Atlanta area."* You do. Now when you introduce yourself to new potential clients, you use your pitch.

The next step in the "Idea" phase is to test the validity of your idea by bringing a sample, a trial, a prototype, early service, etc., to the market to assess the response. Your mentor is a big proponent of "going to market." You have already done this, since you have been selling Molly's Pops on the weekend for the last eight months. Since you had also been contemplating focusing your efforts in the area of events, parties and meetings, she suggested you start to network within the community to gauge the response and to get a sense of price points and ways you might package your product and services, offering add-ons to bump up profits. By selling to the events market, you were not only offering a product, you were also offering a service: décor. More than that, you were planning to tailor the product to the event itself. If the customer wanted red, white and blue pops for the mayor's office by July 3rd, you could provide that. Because of the boutique nature of the personal service you plan to offer, your mentor suggested you look into pricing. You should probably charge more for personalized services.

You can see why it is important to get to market with your idea, because only the marketplace will tell you if you have something of value that others want to buy. It is important to listen to the marketplace as there might be opportunities associated with your product or service of which you were not aware but that you can take advantage of. There might also be pitfalls that you need to avoid.

After all this, are you still feeling energized by your idea? Are you ready for the huge amount of work a new business guarantees? By this stage, you should be brimming with excitement. You really feel that you have a great idea and you are onto something. You are buzzing. And any doubts that you have, you can work through or around. Your decision tree has opened your eyes to potential pitfalls and turned them into challenges. You are raring to take your idea and build it into a business.

GirlPreneurship, here you come!

The Goal-Setting Phase

Name: Carly O. and Avery
Business: Lights Out Productions, Inc.
Location: Toronto, ON
Age: 33

It's 5 a.m. and the alarm is going off and I try to remember that I love being the boss and I really do want to head into the office before everyone else, way before everyone else, to get a jump on the day like I usually do. At this hour, I'm hardly convincing, but I get up anyway and head to the kitchen for a few reviving gulps of coffee from my pre-set pot before showering. I read the notes I wrote myself last night on my chalkboard wall: "Get coffee, grab a coat, go make a film!" Yeah, I'm funny when there is free time and I have nothing to do but write myself notes on the chalkboard. I do this on the days I know I'll need a kick in the pants. Below my note to self, I've made a basic outline of the day. In the early morning, seeing my schedule scribbled out like this gives me the visual assurance I need. I can see the day and start to task it out in my mind. Visual person and all, you know. When

I get into the office, I already know what's on. It's just something I do when I'm really busy, especially when we've got a few projects going at once and time is precious, and time is money.

That's why setting goals is crucial to your success as a GirlPreneur. You're in business to create something, to carve out your niche in the economy and your time is valuable. And that means setting and having goals to know you are getting somewhere. Use your calendar and organizer. Get into the habit of looking at the tasks for the day, the week and the month. Divide up complicated work into manageable parts. Delegate the busy work if you can. And set deadlines, even if they are artificial ones. If you don't, the work can drag on. It's amazing how making a deadline, even an artificial one, can motivate you.

Seven years ago, when my friend Avery and I started our film production company, Lights Out Productions, Inc., we mapped out where we wanted to be in 1 year, 2 years and 5 years. We knew that the first few years were going to make or break us. It was crucial to identify the company's goals on a daily, weekly and monthly basis. And it was critical for both of us to take a very active role in client relations and project management. Since I was the director and Avery the producer, it seemed as if there would be a natural division of labour. But for the time being, we both needed to bring in clients. Each of us had our networks. Every Friday we met to go over what had happened during the week, and discuss what was coming up.

We were lucky enough to have great interns from the city's film school who helped us immensely. They acquired work experience and we got people to do a lot of the busy work. We were able to establish nice routines. If we weren't in production, Mondays and Fridays were devoted to meeting with potential new clients. The other days I was usually working on scripts, and pitching ideas to broadcasters and distributors.

My creative process is to scribble in notebooks. Instead of keying things into a laptop or a smartphone, I keep notebooks that I always carry around. It may sound unorganized and sloppy, but it works for me. These notebooks usually last several months; as soon as one is full, I buy a new one. The old notebooks are kept in a file on a shelf in case I need to refer back to something. I take notes at all meetings. It's personal preference. We all have our own methods and materials that we like to use.

It's important to look at your company goals through two different lenses: the big picture goals and the small picture goals—also called the macro and the micro goals. The big picture goals might be six months to five years away whereas the small picture goals might be from today to 6 months from now. With the macro view, you are projecting where you want your company to be in the years ahead. With the micro goals, you are looking at the incremental tasks that will be required to reach each goal. You are making big goals and breaking them down into small action steps. If you complete your small-picture goals, the ones that you set for yourself every day, you will be one step closer to reaching your big-picture goals.

Today the list reads: 1. Find distribution deal for in-house films. 2. Discuss rights to in-house films to large network prospect. 3. Continue to graze for private sources of funding for our independent films. 4. Explore foreign distribution channels for in-house catalogue. And so on.

Setting goals allows you to plan in the present for how you intend to have your future unfold. And it's a way to keep reminding ourselves of where we are going and how we are going to get there. Having it on paper in front of you keeps it clear and static even as the world around us keeps moving. Goal setting keeps you focused and accountable.

Every holiday season, I take two weeks off. One week is reserved for my family, the other, I spend reflecting on the previous year's business. Then I look at the coming year and give it a name. Last year was The Year of the New Director. And it was! We contracted two new directors for two films we made that year and they were both fantastic. They pulled out great performances from the actors

Confessions of a GirlPRENEUR | 115

and brought a polished commercial appeal to the films. It didn't hurt that one of the directors is married to a very well-known actress who was willing to work as the lead for way less than her usual fee. We got lucky with that one. The film is now being distributed by one of the hottest L.A. indie distributors and we're looking at box office revenue in the upper millions. It is turning out to be one of those unexpected small films (the budget was a few million) that goes on to become a box office hit. All the attention has opened up a few doors to some other lucrative projects. So our goal of working with a few new directors paid off. But you never know. Nothing is ever a sure thing, especially in a transient business like film production.

As an entrepreneur, it is essential to keep your finger on the financial pulse of your business so that you know when you need to pivot—when to adjust your course of action, company goals or overall vision so that you can stay on track. You may need to modify, add, delete, scale up or scale down immediately. This is a natural process in the survival and growth of any business. In fact, most businesses spend the first years in survive-to-thrive mode. The real test is how your idea fares in the marketplace. And if the marketplace indicates that you are on the wrong path via poor sales, you will need to pivot—and pivot quickly.

Here is an example of pivoting from my own experiences a few years back. We were right out of film school and, the film part aside, struggling to manage a business as we went along. Even though our original mission was to make inspiring films, we had to pay the bills. We started making very low-budget commercials and web content for local businesses and any organizations that would hire us. One of us had a family member who owned a chain of local cafes, and we had landed a contract with him. Because the commercial and web content work seemed like a profitable direction, we had been concentrating our efforts on finding similar clients.

But always with "real" film ideas in the backs of our minds. What we ended up doing was typical. We financed a low-budget film ourselves. When we weren't busy with the commercial work, we wrote the script, called in favours, put together a crew and shot the film and made a low-budget movie. The result was luck plus industry. That film ended up pivoting the company back towards its original mission. The film got press. It didn't make a lot of money, but it made enough for us to finance a few other films, so that when the New Director film came along we were able to take a chance. Because by that time we had a track record and some good press.

We put a lot of time and passion and our own money into the making of that first film. Lots of people have made small films, and some of those have even received great acclaim, but not

Confessions of a GirlPRENEUR | 117

enough to propel those filmmakers into feature length filmmaking. It can take years to get a film made. We got lucky. But we also did what we had to do to make it work. We had set goals that we were always aiming for, and when we had the chance we pivoted and took advantage of opportunities.

So you see, goal-setting can be a highly motivating process as well as an effective tool for mapping the road to success.

Things to consider when setting goals:

- ✓ Identify your goals.
- ✓ Divide them into macro-goals and micro-goals. Macro – decide on the big picture goals or where you want your company to be in 1 year, 2 years, 5 years, etc. Micro – break down the yearly goals into more manageable time frames such as quarterly, monthly, weekly and daily.
- ✓ Measure your goals.
- ✓ Chart your progress and be accountable.
- ✓ Affirm your goals.
- ✓ Constantly revisit your goals and even say them out loud. I am a firm believer that you become what you believe.
- ✓ Execute on your goals.
- ✓ Get out there and work. Get as much done in a day as possible. Check those daily goals off the list when you've achieved them!

✓ Adapt your goals. When circumstances change or opportunities arise, review where you want to be, taking the new conditions into consideration and pivot. Pivot if necessary. Don't be afraid to alter your course to get your business back on track.

Above all—have fun! Being a GirlPreneur is hard work, but few things in life are as rewarding as working for yourself.

Your Business Plan

Name: **Alice and Janey**
Business: **Cyched Out Bike Shop**
Location: **Portland, Oregon**
Age: **41 and 42**

My friend Alice and her partner Janey own The Cyched Out Bike Shop in Portland, Oregon, where outdoor recreation is very in. The city boasts loads of bike paths, bike-friendly roads and mountain trails on which to spend the day trekking. They opened the store when Portland was becoming a hub for the young and the restless and have since become part of the neighbourhood culture.

How did they do this? By creating a hotspot for people who were looking for excellence in biking. They knew the market and how to position their business: they sell high-end products to outdoorsy, eco-friendly, dog-loving people who prefer to buy locally and believe it's important to know the names of their bike repair people. Customer loyalty is a big deal here and Cyched Out has earned a place in the bike lovers' hearts.

But the business wasn't an immediate success. Alice and Janey first opened their doors in a very gritty, artsy area full of lofts and warehouse spaces, one block away from the main drag. The problem was that this location was really terrible. It had seemed well-suited at the time; there were a lot of potential customers in the area, but it turned out that the shop's visibility from the street wasn't good. They had imagined potential customers would wander off the beaten path and find the store easily. To their surprise, they found people really didn't venture off the main shopping street, and they were on the street behind that. The warehouse provided really great space, but even with a sign in the main square pointing in their direction, people still didn't find them. There just wasn't enough foot traffic, and that was the traffic they needed. They wanted to provide biking resources to their neighbourhood and they wanted to see the business grow by word of mouth because that usually meant customer loyalty.

So they kept their eyes out for a better location. During that time, Alice worked at her full-time job as a director of a non-profit while Janey kept up with the bike industry. It took a year and a half until they found a spot that looked right. The space had big front windows facing onto a main shopping corridor, and it was right beside a park.

There was only one catch that Alice and Janey had not counted on: the new location was not for lease, but rather for sale. The property was an entire building, but the price was reasonable. The two entrepreneurs had to make a decision. They spent a lot of time talking things over and referring back to the business plan they had created years ago.

The partners had strategically mapped out how they were going to create a cycling hotspot for years to come. Their vision was to offer a lot more than just bikes. As part of their store's strategy to engage with the biking community, they would hire the best-trained service techs in the industry. In addition to fixing bikes, they would offer bike maintenance classes and cycling seminars on evenings and weekends. In their original plan, Alice had also proposed opening a bike café. And if they were going to own the building, the income from the rentals could allow a small renovation on the ground-level space to open out toward the park for a terraced café. She knew through both research and personal experience that cyclists are a special breed. They liked to meet and talk, they loved to share information. They were great gossips! The Cyched Out Coffee Shop would give all those bike lovers a place to go before or after their 30-kilometre treks. They could drink matcha-soy lattes and talk about the latest high-priced gruppos while their kids ran around.

So Alice and Janey bought the property and renovated the entire ground level to include a shop, a café and even living quarters for themselves. They love it and business is good. Sales last year were $1 million. The bike shop was running at a profit of 30%. The coffee shop was netting $250K in profits.

Here is the original business plan for the Cyched Out Bike Shop. This is purely a template for you to understand the five core components to develop a business plan for your venture:

Executive Summary:

We are positioning ourselves to become Portland's one stop bike shop for biking needs. Our products are top of the line, and our service technicians are the best. As owners and cycling enthusiasts, we have formed a partnership for a long-term business. Our shop will be located in a prominent shopping area that caters to the local community and in the future we plan to open a café adjacent to the shop to provide a meeting place and an educational center offering biking seminars and maintenance classes. Our business model consists of down-to-earth, informative, friendly and personal service alongside an unparalleled retail and educational experience.

Our Mission:

At Cyched Out Bike Shop we are going to provide this vibrant community with the best possible, most up-to-date full-scale retail sales of new bicycles and parts, accessories, clothing and gear while also providing excellent personalized maintenance and repair services and educational opportunities.

Our Objectives:

We will:

- ✓ Provide high quality sales and service in a premier highly-visible location.
- ✓ Maintain a financially healthy business with 30% net profit margins.
- ✓ Achieve monthly and yearly sales objectives and review these monthly.
- ✓ Provide the best lines of biking clothing and accessories in visually interesting displays.
- ✓ Offer biking-related seminars taught by biking gurus in the community.
- ✓ Focus marketing on new groups each month. One month university students. Next month families. Next month workers downtown.

Our Strategies:

Our location is part of our strategy. We want to eventually purchase a unique location in the urban core. We are the only bike shop currently offering extensive high quality equipment and personalized repair. Our biking seminars will be the best. Our relationships are part of our strategy. We develop long lasting personal relationships within the cycling community. Our commitment is part of our strategy.

Action Plan:

We will listen to our customers' needs and to feedback from the community. We will each spend two to three hours a day spreading the word about our business. We will participate on the board of directors of cycling associations and in local community civic affairs. The shop will have unparalleled bike service repair techs. The shop will have creative visual merchandising. A good accountant will watch the financial metrics and know our numbers. We will be open to opportunities and pivot if need be. We will create Cyched Out Bike Shop T-shirts that President Obama will wear on his next bike tour with Cyched Out Bike Tours! That last one is the vision of the future!

The importance of a business plan is that it grounds you in the reality of your circumstances. In the early stages, you don't need a ten-plus-page business plan and you don't need to hire a costly consultant to create one for you. You need to focus on the execution of your idea so that you can get yourself out the door to start selling and bringing in customers and revenue!

Your plan should be simple, clear and concise. Don't strive for perfection at this stage but rather understand the concept: clearly refine your idea (problem and solution), make your decision, set your goals, and create a plan to reach your goals.

Your business plan is written by you for you. It is a tool to understand how your business will be built. There is no right or wrong way of writing the plan; however, it should focus on how you are going to achieve your macro and micro goals, how you will monitor your progress, all aspects of your sales and marketing vision, staffing and so on.

Although all businesses are different and will require different business plans, as your business starts to take off and moves from survive to thrive in rapid time, you can start to get more rigorous and write separate and very detailed plans for each of the categories above. But for now, don't get lost in the details. Focus on having a clear idea and a clear plans for bringing your idea to market.

Your focus almost from the moment that you decide to jump in and become a GirlPreneur is getting to market! Now you are ready to build your company by being a lean, mean marketing and sales machine while delivering the highest quality product or service!

The Art of Marketing and Sales

Name:	**Serena**
Business:	**Cherry Orchard Beer**
Location:	**Manitoulin Island, ON**
Age:	**23**

"Marketing and sales" is your mantra. Why? Because as a successful GirlPreneur, you know that engaging and retaining your customers is key. It's a busy, chaotic marketplace out there, one that requires an exceptional effort to get your business known. To stand out, you must be passionate and care about what you are doing. Passionate energy will carry over into what you create, how you perform and how you relate to others, and into the quality of the product or service you are selling. You must inject your passion and creativity into every aspect of marketing: product development, customer service, advertising, packaging, display, distribution and networks.

Marketing is the art of creating an original brand that has a compelling story and then effectively getting the word out. Think about the strengths of your product or service. What's your edge? How is it different from the competition? Look at your competitive analysis. Zero in on the strengths and qualities of what you are offering, then market it using those angles.

Selling is the art of identifying, understanding and appealing to your customer base. Customers buy the promises, the solutions, the prestige—whatever they believe your product will deliver. Your customers must believe they are getting value for their money. If you can convince a customer that your brand is authentic, if you can make her believe in what your company stands for, then you will have earned customer loyalty.

This is especially true with certain products. Take microbrewed beer. Serena had been living on Manitoulin Island for 10 years. She had always loved craft beer. She regularly travelled to craft beer festivals, where she ended up talking to the brewers at length. Several times a year she visited the microbreweries that were making a name for themselves. When she heard about a grant program through the government for start-up businesses that focused on local artisanal products, she applied, explaining that she wanted to open a small, in-house microbrewery she would name Cherry Orchard.

Manitoulin Island is a small community. Cherry trees grow wild in the area and Serena would often spend July weekends gathering the fruit before the crows got to it. Even before she heard about the grant, she had been using the cherries to brew beer in her kitchen. After experimenting with recipes and asking friends to act as tasters, she finally mixed a brew that she found exceptional—very dark, very citrusy, with a cherry tone. It appealed to both men and women since it wasn't sweet but had, like the cherries themselves, both a sweet and a tart edge. People in the area had started to stop her in the grocery store and ask her where they could buy some. Word had gotten out about Cherry Orchard beer.

Studies have shown that people often make buying decisions based on emotions and how the brand makes them feel. So you need to persuade customers that your product or service is the one that they can feel good about buying. They must feel they have gotten good value for their money. Appeal to your customers by standing for something they find relevant and enriching. Determine the value price point. Give your customer a "message" that motivates them to try your product or service, and if you have created something they believe is of quality and is cost effective, you will most likely win them over.

In other words, a successful sales and marketing plan aims to persuade the buyer into believing

Confessions of a GirlPRENEUR | 129

that your product or service—your brand—fulfills their needs and wants. Great branding can give you an edge in the marketplace.

Serena knew a local beer could do well. People here are proud of their heritage. A beer brewed from the harvests of the island would be something special—if the beer was good, that is. If the product was good and the price was decent, she knew the people here would stand behind it.

Serena got a loan for capital investment in her microbrewery for the Manitoulin Island region. Since she had already been brewing and bottling in her home, she had a brew mix that was working. Now she needed to think about turning her hobby into an actual business. She decided to keep her teaching job for the time being, to see how things went. She would brew on weekends and distribute her product herself after school in her truck, and think about marketing and keeping track of the financials on week-nights. This meant she had to give up her bowling group and her Thursday night pub hang outs, as she was too busy now to do much else besides focus on the logistics of getting her microbrewery up and running.

The Cherry Orchard brand had a good story. The island. The cherry orchards. The mill that harnessed the power of water and provided electricity to the factory where she set up her small brewery for very little capital output. The mill was looking for tenants and offering cheap rents for those who would keep the place up. As a single woman brewing beer in a sparsely-inhabited part of the country, her story was interesting. The design on the labels was a photograph of the old orchard on the front with the story of the beer on the back.

Her marketing strategy was based around her personal story and the heritage of the island itself. Her brand became about the place, the people, the customs and the landscape of the island. When the time came to market her products to the surrounding communities, she found that people had already heard of her brew, and Cherry Orchard beer already had a name that preceded the marketing campaign. But she had spent time perfecting the brew, the actual product. By the time, she went to market in a real way, she had the advantage of word of mouth. She'd achieved a consistent look and logo and was delivering a consistent level of quality product on time.

Her sales strategy was to get her beer placed in the local pubs first. She knew most of the proprietors, which was a big help. But figuring out pricing, the brewing schedule and the product delivery schedules was a new puzzle. She had a hard time with that. Finally, she admitted that she needed to bring in a consultant to help her because she knew she couldn't tell her pub customers that she didn't have enough product to deliver. Keeping her reputation relied on her consistency of delivery.

Confessions of a GirlPRENEUR | 131

Selling is an art that can be practised. Take a look at what Serena learned about marketing and sales in the steps below. You know what they say—practice makes perfect.

Serena's Exceptional Sales and Marketing Tool Kit:

- ✓ Sparkle! Smile! People love passionate people. Your enthusiasm will be contagious!
- ✓ Be on your game all the time. GirlPreneurship is a lifestyle.
- ✓ Be honest about the product or service you are selling.
- ✓ Always be professional and polished.
- ✓ Be sharp. Know your business inside and out. Speak with authority, sincerity and pizzazz.
- ✓ See everyone as a customer. See every customer as a gateway to a network.
- ✓ Create a culture of excellence. People rise to their potential.
- ✓ Be outstanding and expect others around you to be as well.
- ✓ Practice goodwill and give back to your community. A lot.
- ✓ Have fun! Even when it gets tough, keep focused on all the awesome things about being a GirlPreneur!

There is no single way to approach a marketing and sales strategy. The strategy for your business will be part of an ongoing evaluation process that is specific to your company. However, there are core principles that can help you determine the direction of your strategies and the necessary tactics to employ to drive sales and keep customer loyalty. It is important to differentiate yourself from your competitors. You will have a competitive edge just by virtue of being passionate about your product or service and, by extension, by having the desire to show the world how great the product or service is and how it can enrich people's lives, boost their company's reputation, etc.

Points to keep in mind to find out what strategy suits your particular business:

- ✓ Your market envelopment strategy. How will you proceed to enter, secure and seize your share of the marketplace?
- ✓ The current market. How well do you know it?
- ✓ Your growth strategy. What percentage of the market do you aim to capture now and in the future?
- ✓ Your media strategy. How will you use different forms of media to your advantage?
- ✓ Your distribution channels. Will you have self-distribution, a dedicated sales team, or an outside sales rep/distribution company?
- ✓ Your communications strategy. Will you tweet? Or hire someone to set up your social media? Every business must have

a website these days to promote powerful online engagement for your brand.
- ✓ Your competition. Who are your rivals in the business? How are you holding out in terms of market share?
- ✓ Your market position. What position are you aiming for?

Cherry Orchard eventually expanded to include four additional seasonal brews that changed slightly each year but always used the fruits and products of the island along with wild herbs and traditional spices. Although distribution channels had been complicated to organize, first-year sales exceeded expectations.

On a personal level, Serena spent the year so immersed in the business she neglected physical fitness and really wanted to get back to Pilates. It would take another year before she felt she had the time. Those first few years, she concentrated on securing suppliers that she trusted, setting up contracts and working with the scheduling consultant. There was a lot to learn about and a lot to do. There were also grants to apply for, billing systems to put into place and inventory to manage.

Into the second year, she started teaching part time because her full-time job didn't allow her the time she needed to work on the business. There were so many decisions to make. She was dealing with so many things—labels, tap handles, emails, contests, beer events. Midway through the year, Serena invested in a portable beer garden that she used at events. She hired a man named Jack as a full-time beer ambassador to work at most of the large and small festivals in the province and slightly beyond.

Jack turned out to be a great hire. He was a whiz at math, scheduling and social media, and he pushed the brand out there. Sales at festivals covered Jack's salary and the garden supplies and materials. The beer garden was worth it as a marketing tool. Jack even entered the Orchard's Pear with Pepper label in a contest run by a national beer association. The paper labels, sepia-toned and printed with soy inks, had a nice feel and look. The label placed third and got a mention in a beer newsletter. Any press the beer received reinforced the visual recognition of the brand. And Jack kept the name out in the social media on Twitter and wrote a monthly blog about their brews, including customers' stories from the beer garden tours. But the best form of advertising for Cherry Orchard was its followers talking about how much they loved the product.

Serena found that sales and marketing were a part of the business that she really felt comfortable with and continued to enjoy. There were other parts of the business where she needed professional help. In addition to Jack, she had an accountant who did the financials and reports, and she hired a

Confessions of a GirlPRENEUR | 135

local teenager to help clean the facility. Everything else she and Jack handled.

She even continued to self-distribute. She knew this was a very important part of the sales strategy, since no one else could talk about her beer better than she could. And by doing this she saved the 30% wholesaler's margin. She loved to get out and visit her clients and found that they loved it too. She found that she could sell them far more product than what they had initially wanted. She joined the beer associations, she started partnerships with festivals and events, first locally, then slowly province-wide and beyond. She started to consider whether she wanted to grow the company and what her strategy would be.

The power of Serena's story or those of GirlPreneurs like her is that they understand how critical it is to get in front of customers to sell. Her passion for her product turned her into a dynamic sales person. Serena knew that sales was at the core of getting her business off the ground.

A GirlPreneur's Trade Secrets in Marketing and Sales

Name: Serena (Cont'd)
Business: Cherry Orchard Beer
Location: Manitoulin Island, ON
Age: 23

At the trade shows she attended, Serena was often asked to share her marketing and sales tips. She enjoyed formalizing them and talking about them with others who were contemplating opening their own small brew enterprises. These are the principles that she shared:

- ✓ Love your brand and your product or service. This is paramount. If you don't enjoy selling—after all, not all entrepreneurs are salespeople—then hire someone who will passionately sell for you.
- ✓ Know your product or service. Go back to the idea phase and recite the business idea pitch you perfected in 30 seconds or less. Guess what? You're going to be using that

sharp, focused and concise pitch a lot when you're out there talking about your company, explaining what you are doing and why potential customers want to buy from you. And know the details of the competition's product or service and how yours distinguishes itself.

✓ Be passionate about what you're selling—even on bad days when you are grumpy and your cat is grumpy too. Passion creates a buzz and sparks the potential customer's interest and promotes engagement.

✓ Adapt your pitch to your customer base. Sales is about knowing your customers and their potential needs. Serena approached pub owners differently than festival organizers. They needed different information and were geared towards different things. Adapt your style to the person in front of you. Taking the time to know your clients and learn how they engage is imperative when selling.

✓ Pace yourself. Know when to apply the right amount of pressure to encourage a sale. Know when to pull back to give someone space.

✓ Learn the art of persistence. In a complex marketplace, constant and consistent messaging can be critical to success. A sale is rarely made at the first point of contact. Several points of contact, or more, are often needed to secure a sale. As a GirlPreneur, it is your persistence that pays off.

✓ Keep the dialogue with a potential customer open-ended. Don't force a yes or no answer.

✓ Pitch the advantages of your product or service versus what is out there. Be forward. Be outrageous. Be engaging. Be *you*!

✓ Give something away. Have something you can give to customers, such as a sample or a post card. The more we see an advertisement for a brand, the more familiar it becomes and the more likely we are to reach for it at purchase time because we already feel an affinity for it.

✓ Acknowledge and utilize the power of testimonials. Few tactics are more effective than a former or existing customer's endorsement. Be bold and ask for referrals.

The Confessions

My biggest confession is that no one is more surprised than me that I became as successful in business as I did, where I was able to retire at 42 years old with a nice pile of cash in the bank and a little leather-bound black book of boyfriends. There were many days when I didn't feel smart enough, savvy enough or even qualified enough to end up here. But when you're in the thick of it, you don't realize how much sheer stamina and determination count for. It was only when I started to get gigs on the speaking circuit that I began to realize that I had achieved something quite difficult. And, especially, since often I was one of only a few female founders speaking at these events. And that, my friends, was partly why I wanted to write this book.

In the height of those company-building years, I was always immersed in business. There was not much time to contemplate how I was doing it. There were only things to get done, ASAP. I spent my life being busy doing and building things, and hardly ever sitting and reflecting on the sum of it all. Only in the last couple of years, since my kids are older and I've been out meeting other business folks, have I seen the splash I've made in the pond. I've always seen myself as the geeky girl riding around on my bike, no cool factor involved.

I've learned all kinds of things in writing this book. In fact, I've had to go to confession for my own soul. Of course, walking down memory lane was fun, recounting all those childhood memories. And the business part of the book was easy to talk about as well—about the drive and step-by-step processes and being meticulous and keeping the balance sheet in the black, which now seems second nature.

Being an entrepreneur has been incredibly rewarding. I wouldn't change any part of my journey. Ok, maybe the divorce part. But missteps, mistakes and challenges are all a part of who we become. Confessing them is not to deter you but rather inspire you to beat the odds by not just presenting a rosy picture of success. For any story to have true value, we need to share our successes with our mistakes.

But what did I know of those other topics on the cover of the book—of matters of the heart? Love: what have I learned of love, you might ask? Or babies? Or life in general? And this was where the work of writing this book became, well, difficult. I was a social worker turned entrepreneur

Confessions of a GirlPRENEUR | 141

with my head down; a workaholic in the business of helping people. I didn't take the time to foster much else away from my desk. You see, I was far from the poster child for success in my personal life or love life, definitely not.

But let's start with the confessions; in a way a sort of cautionary tale, in the hopes that you might glean something from my experiences.

Confession #1

As a young woman, I was so driven to prove something that a crazy cycle of achieving ensued, which served me well in business, but not so much in my personal life.

My father's early death had been a wake-up call. There I was having just graduated from university, and I not only lost my cherished father, but I saw my mom lose her husband. Thankfully she had a career that would protect her financially, and many interests that would allow her to continue to remain busy in the absence of her relationship. Witnessing this gave me the drive to make sure I could take care of myself. Life was unpredictable, I was discovering yet again.

I was an over-achiever who lost her father, then lost her first career job, and I admit I ended up shell-shocked for a while. When I started my business, everything became about making a nest egg for myself, about protecting myself. A career seemed a safer choice to put a roof over my head and money in the bank account than did a relationship.

During that time, it seems that I let slip that part of me that could connect to others in an intimate, meaningful way. I put myself on overdrive with goals in mind and I didn't look back. I was more comfortable 'doing' than 'being' and I was really good at doing. The result was my personal life suffered at a time when paying attention to it would be crucial in setting the trajectory for the rest of my life.

If I had taken the time for some self-reflection, maybe I would have figured out that I could have done both well, business and love. Sure, when I was a GirlPreneur, I had some boyfriends, and I loved the buzz and fun of dating, but I would invariably wake up the next morning and hit the gym then go to the office and that was that. My drive and ambitions always ended up winning my attention for the long haul.

This was my reality. Looking back, I recognize that the more successful I became, the less of an ability I had to be emotionally intimate in a relationship. But yours can be different. It just takes reminding and a level of discipline to shut the lights off and go switch gears into your personal life. Maintaining a balance requires self-awareness and discipline.

Confession #2

At the time, what I failed to realize was that success is only one part of the happiness equation. You can have all the money in the world, but be alone and unhappy. Conversely, you can have little money but lots of friends, and be quite content.

It was my entrepreneurial spirit combined with fear and shell-shock that drove me to only focus on business to the exclusion of other parts of my life. And that is where I lost the balance between the personal and the entrepreneurial.

But let's back up. What about that 'fallen in love' part that I mentioned earlier? Well…let me give you my (very) short story on the two men that took my heart.

Before I started my business, when I was in my early twenties, I had been the fun girl who loved to flirt, date, have fun and spend endless hours in pursuit of these. And guys, well, they were my weakness. And then one day a special one came along. He was my first true love, this wonderful guy that I ended up dating for five years. We were best friends with the hots and nobody knew me better than he did and vice versa. There were no conversations that were off limits. We were truly in love and he was the guy I probably should have married. Maybe I was too young and believed that there would be an endless path of 'falling in love.' Maybe the timing wasn't right. I don't really remember, but I did end up being the one to end the relationship.

A number of years after that, my children's father came along. All I can say is that the minute we met, it was explosive love at first sight. We shared a passion for fun, music, food and travel that would outlast us. It was a tumultuous relationship based on a love between two strong people who just didn't want the same things from life. Without sharing the details of the fine line that exists between lovers and the drama that unfolds, we parted ways, but we have two amazing daughters as a result of our time together.

Those are my stories about falling in love. I'm imparting what wisdom I have earned, slight though it might be; the thing I will say, is being in love is wonderful while it lasts.

Confession #3

I think men are fantastic. Maybe some more than others, but still… Like I have said, I was a girl who sought out fun guys who brought out that side of me to offset my more serious, ambitious side and help me relax and tone down. Being with this type of man was like being on a mini-holiday from myself. They didn't ask a whole lot from me which made them even more attractive.

It was a comedy of errors in a way. In the early years as an entrepreneur the responsibility, stress and worry is high-pitched. I avoided picking personal partners that demanded an emotional connection, even though that very connection is needed for two people to grow together. If the only talking that's happening is over a pillow, then chances are the depth of that connection will be, let's say, limited.

So like everything in life, there is always a flip side. And with these boyfriends, their common denominator was that they most often lacked the DNA chip for responsibility. And yes, many of them were educated professionals that loved their mother's and what have you. But when it came to relationships, it was unlikely that they were going to settle down and make stellar husbands and fathers.

If it is your inclination and you are keen on finding a partner while acing it as a GirlPreneur, it's probably a good idea to consider your mate's qualifications for the job. I mean, you are an amazing girl with a lot on the go. Whoever gets to ride the wave with you, had best be up to par.

You can date the 'bad' boys and have fun with them, but for goodness sakes, don't marry them or make them long-term partners. Some do mature into the role, but is that a chance you really want to take? Rarely will someone change because you want them to. No amount of talking, fighting and ultimatums can convince someone to love you or change for you if they do not want to. The person you see is the person you get.

If I knew then what I know now, I might have made different choices. And no, I don't have regrets, because I do believe that life is a journey filled with mistakes and lessons learned along the way. Think clearly with your head and your heart as much about your personal life and the decisions you make to move it forward as you do with your business life.

Be smart, be selective, know you are worth it. Don't settle for less than what you want and deserve. Ever.

Confession #4

Choosing your personal partner is one of *the* most important decisions you'll make. It's a very important issue for GirlPreneurs when considering the possibility of not only nurturing a business, but nurturing children as well, if you want to combine being a powerhouse GirlPreneur / Female Founder with being a mother. In order to pull it all off and not go stark raving mad from the demands placed on you, you need to be supported.

Pick someone who will notice that there are no groceries in the house and will go and buy some!

Confessions of a GirlPRENEUR | 147

That dinner is in an hour and you're not home, so time for them to get cooking. Someone who is willing to prioritize your needs with their own and has the maturity to place your needs ahead of friends, golf games, and nights out. Someone who, when you call them because your head is in a toilet suffering from morning sickness, will drop what they are doing and you won't even have to ask. They will love you that much that you are their priority. And in return, you will soar because you have found someone that you can rely on in life while you're out there building your beautiful business.

Confession #5

As entrepreneurs, we work too much. In fact, I'm still guilty of it. I know we've said it before, but it is the running theme in the life of an entrepreneur, so I thought it deserved its own confession line. It is nearly impossible to build a company without working long hours. This is a huge advantage to your company but there may be fallout in your personal life.

So, how do you work this out? If you are single and super busy as an entrepreneur, outsource household tasks so that any free time you have you can take for yourself to relax and recharge. If you are in a relationship, it can get tricky, but with love comes compromise. If you have picked a true partner, they will pull their fair share on the home front. This will likely require some negotiation to figure out who does what so that it does not fall to you by default as the female. We don't need to say this of course, but you will need to stand back and not step in to do more than your fair share. Nor will you be critical of your partner's way of emptying the dishwasher, doing the groceries, changing diapers and so on. And even better, if you are both super busy, maybe you can hire out some of the tasks and spend more time relaxing together.

Having a stable happy personal life can be wonderful for a GirlPreneur, whether you are single or with a partner.

Confession #6

Having children is a *very big deal*! In fact, it is, literally, a **huge** deal!

Like many girls, when I was younger I would watch romantic movies and dream about the day I would have children. We would spend endless hours talking about having children and being mothers, but of course we didn't have a clue what we were talking about. We got many of our ideas from television and Hollywood, and how realistic is that. I had been around kids and had babysat, so I knew that having kids would change my life, but until I had my own I didn't realize how much.

Being a GirlPreneur and a mother are not mutually exclusive. You CAN do both. Just know, that life fundamentally changes after children are born. I love my girls more than life itself and motherhood is the most awesome journey, but from the moment I became pregnant everything changed. Not better or worse, just different. Your body changes. Emotions change. Energy changes. Ambitions change. Everything changes!

And a woman's vulnerability increases, because now your life is not your own as your children completely and fully depend upon you. I was fortunate that my company was well established before I had children and this very fact will work to a GirlPreneur's advantage. It is much easier to keep a good company going than to be in the early hustling years as a startup founder. When you become a new mother, you will not have swaths of unlimited time and energy to apply to your company. Even if you have a wonderful, amazing partner or great childcare, you will still be heavily (and rightfully) distracted by new parenthood. Starting and building the momentum for a business requires time, energy and resources.

If you can, take the time before babies come along to invest in yourself by getting your company up and profitable. The sacrifices you make in the early startup years will pay off in dividends once you become a mother. Why? Because you will hopefully be able to step back from business for the time that you need to focus on your baby, without your business crashing down around you. You will keep a watchful eye on business…as baby now becomes your new startup!

Confession #7

Where babies are concerned, the best-laid plans can run amuck. While I was pregnant, I read all the baby books and blogs so that when the baby arrived all I would need was my newfound parental knowledge and everything would be fine. I had built an industry-leading company—how hard could it be to deal with a baby?! I approached this stage of life like any business girl would, with diligence, care and planning. I was used to being able to make things happen by implementing smart processes and practices.

Was I a bit delusional and naive? Yes!

I learned that my baby didn't give a hoot about my resourceful blog reading, the organized shelves of nappies, or the fact that I just needed my coffee to be hot in the morning. I needed parental advice. I started asking questions of every mom I could find: How do you make a baby sleep? How do you make a baby nurse on demand? How? How? How?

The answer: there are no definitive answers. And that I had to accept. Welcome to motherhood. My 8.3 pound beautiful baby became the CEO of *me*!

Confession #8

Motherhood is an extreme sport. My pre-baby GirlPreneur schedule now turned into a series of mad dashes. Because I was nursing, I would go into the office in brief spurts—three or four a day—while functioning on a few hours of sleep. Although, I had taken the time to prepare the company for my maternity leave, I learned within a few weeks of baby's arrival that it was very difficult to replace my role. My team was young and dynamic, but as the founder my role was to bring the sum of all parts of the business together. My maternity leave evaporated before my eyes.

There I was with my gorgeous baby, in the throes of attachment parenting, and realizing that there was no time off for this GirlPreneur turned new mother. Although I was now working mostly from home, I was always plugged into the office. My baby needed me. My business needed me. I had to learn, and fast, to balance it all. I was now in a marathon with regular sprints.

And how do we do it? We just do! We learn the art of flexibility, adaptability and going with the flow…the exact qualities a successful GirlPreneur needs to combine business with babies.

Confession #9

And that brings me to my next soul-exposing confession—that it was very difficult to ask for help because I felt that it was a personal short-coming or failure if I couldn't manage it all and make it look easy. And many entrepreneurs are wired this way. Pride and ego can be our own worst enemies.

Yet behind the visages of many successful female founders are young GirlPreneurs who live in perpetual states of exhaustion because they are doing so much on their own: trying to meet overhead costs, hustling for new clients, building new products and just trying to make a profit. Yes, we love what we do, building our dreams and not someone else's, but in hindsight many of us have learned that it is okay—actually more than okay…essential!—to ask for support. But you have to ask.

There are many networks out there that women in business can turn to for support, be it for referrals, services, mentors, sponsors or peer-to-peer friendships.

Confession #10

But as I urge you to reach out, I also share with you a cautionary tale that many female founders (including yours truly) have experienced.

Confessions of a GirlPRENEUR | 153

The majority of funded entrepreneur and business networks are run by men, for men. As such, their comfort zone lies in what they know: male-driven enterprises. The result? They can be unsupportive and even dismissive of GirlPreneur ideas and initiatives simply because our ventures are out of their scope of understanding. The impact is that although you may have a great idea or venture, if you are told early on that your business has no merit, simply because you unknowingly asked the wrong advisors, you could be turned off moving forward as an entrepreneur.

Don't let that happen! You are a smart and savvy entrepreneur with great potential. Follow due diligence before you seek out advisors.

And that is not to say that established female founders have all the answers. We don't! However, we understand that there is a lot of success to be had in what men might dismiss as stereotypical women's businesses—health, beauty, childcare, family.

Honestly, do you think that the guy at the golf course is going to brag about investing in a new blow dry salon franchise or a line of organic beauty products or that there is a new undergarment out there that is guaranteed to make you look 20 years younger? Not likely.

Do your due diligence before you seek out advice. You don't have time to spare or waste. Look for women-run, women-based networks because women will see the opportunity in your venture and will likely be more supportive.

Confession #11

Seeking support in times of need is important. This brings us to the topic of mental health and the GirlPreneur. Knowing the signs of exhaustion, stress, and overload are critical to your longevity in the field.

There is a very fine line between being a healthy overachiever and an unhealthy overachiever. Like many, I never took time off because I was afraid of letting go and I was afraid of failure. But if I had let go even for a small amount of time each day—to go to the gym, to get a massage, to have a relaxing lunch with a friend—I now know looking back that it would not have hurt my business. It would have made it better.

Find confidantes, friends, or anyone you can trust to talk to. Being an entrepreneur is an awesome journey but it is also challenging and at times, frightening. Our mental health is reliant upon our ability to ask for help. There is no shame in asking for professional help either.

Not going stark raving mad and looking after our mental health should be on our annual goals list.

Confession #12

There is no shame as a female founder to tell the world that our children are a priority. By the time of the birth of my second child, my company was well-established in the marketplace and I was starting to realize that I needed some time off to recharge. I made a strategic decision to prioritize my children ahead of my involvement in the day-to-day operations of the company. I could always keep building companies, but I would never again have the chance to spend this time with my children.

My strategy for business was to maintain its beachhead of strong profitability, with no further growth for the next few years. That would allow me to turn over the day-to-day operations to my staff. Sure, I was anxious about letting go of the reins, but it was time to trust that I had hired and trained good people.

I cut back my 80-hour work week to 20 hours, but I was available around the clock. I took my children and my phone everywhere. My office now became the park, the café, or wherever I happened to be. I was still CEO of the company, but I had made the decision to shift the focus, to mostly be at home with my children.

This was not a difficult decision. I was learning that there are ebbs and flows in life. I was keeping a foothold in my company, but my children needed me now.

Confession #13

Going through a divorce, with children and while running a company, was the most difficult thing that I have ever experienced. Never in my wildest dreams did I imagine that this would happen to me and my children. How was I, this successful female founder, finding myself with a personal life in shreds? This was definitely not how I had envisioned my future unfolding when I was a young teenage girl.

The heartache, anguish, turmoil and powerful emotions that occur when we are transitioning out of a long-term relationship are hugely disruptive to our personal and professional lives.

And that's when I did a long and hard life evaluation and came to the conclusion that I'd had a great run in business and it was now time to sell the company. It was time to place focus on my personal life and my children, plus I needed to take care of myself, too. Because I had worked so hard as a GirlPreneur and made many sacrifices while socking away my nest egg, I was able to make a choice: to sell my company, focus on my personal life, and be with my girls.

Confession Wind Down

As we wind down the writing of this book, even though my confessions are far from exhausted, the reality is we have to stop somewhere. A savvy GirlPreneur knows when to hold back and when to move forward. So, this is it folks.

I hope that you have enjoyed the journey as much as we have. That you have had a few chuckles while at the same time reinforcing your determination and skill set to set off for GirlPreneurship.

It's about flying by the seat of your pants and hanging on for the ride. GirlPreneurs are brave. We've made decisions to step outside the box and to blaze our own trail in life; to take on risks while not having any assurance of the outcome.

We worry our mothers and all those around us, but you will have a deep rooted confidence that no matter what, you will succeed, even if it takes a few tries. You are open to the opinions of others yet it's your own voice that guides you.

And while you continue to dream of riches from success and pots of gold at the end of the rainbow, the rewards are in the layering of the small day-to-day accomplishments. Building a business is ultimately a journey of self-discovery as you pass through all of the ups, downs, and sideways moves that are required on the way to your destination.

Take the time to enjoy your journey. Have no regrets. Live your life as if it's the only one you have.

GirlPreneurs, hang on to your knickers for the ride of your life!

Afterword

After all of this, what is happening now? I continue to try to be the best mother that I can be to two amazing girls, and I have also started to return to my roots as a trauma therapist and trainer.

I remain passionate about business as I continue to manage Arranmore Holdings, Inc., my private portfolio company. And I am excited to launch *Confessions of a GirlPRENEUR* to inspire girls and women that entrepreneurship is a great career choice.

I won't ever stop dreaming and living out my passions and ambitions to make a difference in the world. You can take the GirlPreneur out of a business but you can never take the business out of a GirlPreneur.

In gratitude, thank you for reading my story and I wish you much success as you venture forward to live out your ambitions and your dreams through entrepreneurship.

GirlPreneur, your time is now!

About Fiona Gilligan

For more than two decades, Fiona Gilligan has blazed a trail as an entrepreneur, investor and business leader and she now focuses her time to inspire girls and women to become entrepreneurs. Fiona captivates audiences with her story of how a single parent of two small children took a big dream and was able to build up and sell an industry leading company.

Like many entrepreneurs, Fiona's path to success did not follow a normal route. Fiona started her career with a BA in Psychology and a Master of Social Work. After working in child welfare and then the trauma program at a lead trauma hospital, Fiona discovered her gift for entrepreneurship.

As the Founder and CEO (1994-2007) of the Trauma Management Group, Fiona built a revolutionary private business model in trauma care that became an industry leading company in Canada and dealt with disasters such as the World Trade Center, SARS outbreak and the Dawson College shootings.

In addition to founding the Trauma Management Group, Fiona is the owner of Arranmore Holdings, Inc. that specializes in commercial real estate acquisitions, sales and retention of investment properties.

Fiona is a popular speaker and media expert for the advancement of entrepreneurship in women. She is a regular facilitator and presenter at private and public conferences, events and training programs. She is also a two-time nominee for RBC's Top 100 Canadian Women Entrepreneurs.

Fiona is on a mission to inspire more girls and women to become entrepreneurs, while also raising awareness that women entrepreneurs are vital to our local and global economies.

To book Fiona to speak at your next event or to discover more of her ideas, please visit www.fionagilligan.com today.

About Kendall McQueen

Kendall McQueen grew up in a small town in the rolling Blue Ridge Mountains of Virginia where neighbors played banjos on porches and people were always "dropping by." Her career started in Nashville, TN, in the music business. Her first job was with an artist management company, but she quickly moved into filmmaking. She spent the next 12 years working alongside wonderful crews, making award winning music videos for Country Music Television (CMT), VH-1, MTV, with the recording artists of the times, James Taylor, George Jones, Emmylou Harris, Neil Diamond, Allison Krauss, Martina McBride, and many other wonderful singers and bands.

In between music video projects, there were national commercials, TV projects, and documentaries that took her to L.A, to the coast of Maine, and to film locations all over. She also volunteered with professional filmmaking organizations, the Sundance Film Festival, and TIFF (Toronto International Film Festival.)

Confessions of a GirlPRENEUR | 163

Then one day she met a Canadian professor, the next thing she knew they were getting married and moving to Paris, France with their first child. Life became a whirlwind after this. Daughter number two came along and they moved to Nova Scotia then to the Canadian capital, Ottawa. During this time, Kendall became a MomPreneur and volunteer. She leads community initiatives, sits on boards of directors, and volunteers with arts organizations.

She also continues to work on various film projects, a children's show on TVO, a photography documentary series on Knowledge Network, and several made for television movies. In the past 4 years, she has written spec scripts for film production companies.

Look for her blog, DinneratNine.com

Made in the USA
Charleston, SC
22 May 2015